MORE
HOUSES
ARCHITECTS
DESIGN
FOR
THEMSELVES

Architectural Record Books

Affordable Houses
Apartments, Townhouses and Condominiums, 3/e
Architecture 1970-1980: A Decade of Change
The Architectural Record Book of Vacation Houses, 2/e
Buildings for Commerce and Industry
Buildings for the Arts
Contextual Architecture
Energy-Efficient Buildings
Engineering for Architecture
Great Houses for View Sites, Beach Sites, Sites in the Woods,
    Meadow Sites, Small Sites, Sloping Sites, Steep Sites and Flat Sites
Hospitals and Health Care Facilities, 2/e
Houses Architects Design for Themselves
Houses of the West
Institutional Buildings
Interior Spaces Designed by Architects, 2/e
New Life for Old Buildings
Office Building Design, 2/e
Places for People: Hotels, Motels, Restaurants, Bars, Clubs,
    Community Recreation Facilities, Camps, Parks, Plazas and Playgrounds
Public, Municipal and Community Buildings
Religious Buildings
Recycling Buildings: Renovations, Remodelings, Restorations and Reuse
Techniques of Successful Practice
A Treasury of Contemporary Houses
25 Years of Record Houses

Architectural Record Series Books

Ayers: Specifications for Architecture, Engineering and Construction
Feldman: Building Design for Maintainability
Heery: Time, Cost and Architecture
Heimsath: Behavioral Architecture
Hopf: Designer's Guide to OSHA
Portman and Barnett: The Architect As Developer

MORE
HOUSES
ARCHITECTS
DESIGN
FOR
THEMSELVES

AN ARCHITECTURAL RECORD BOOK

Edited by
Walter F. Wagner, Jr., AIA
Editor-in-Chief, *Architectural Record*

McGraw-Hill Book Company

New York
St. Louis
San Francisco
Auckland
Bogotá
Hamburg
Johannesburg
London
Madrid
Mexico

Montreal
New Delhi
Panama
Paris
São Paulo
Singapore
Sydney
Tokyo
Toronto

The articles in this book were written by the editors of
Architectural Record. Acknowledgment is made to *Housing*
magazine for their contributions on the Crites house and the
Bystrom house.

Editors for the book were Patricia Markert and Joan Zseleczky. The
designer was William Bennett. Production supervisors were Carol
Frances, assisted by Susan Stein, and Paul Malchow.

Printed and bound by the Halliday Lithograph Corporation.

1234567890   HDHD   8908765432

Library of Congress Cataloging in Publication Data
Main entry under title:

More houses architects design for themselves.

   "An Architectural record book."
   Articles by the editors of Architectural record.
1. Architect-designed houses — United States.
2. Architects — Homes and haunts — United States.
I. Wagner, Walter F.   II. Architectural Record.
NA7208.M6   728'.0973   81-13695
ISBN 0-07-002365-4   AACR2

MORE
HOUSES
ARCHITECTS
DESIGN
FOR
THEMSELVES

CONTENTS

Introduction:
When architects design houses for themselves and their families

For many families—probably including many readers of this book—a built-for-sale house is not enough. They want a house on a site chosen by them—be it a hillside, a rolling meadow, a close-in and convenient suburban or urban lot—or even high on a mountain or close to the sea. They want a house that meets their specific family needs in a special way—not a house that was designed for "the average homebuyer." They want a house that reflects their particular ideas of beauty; their choices of materials and color and texture and degree of finish. They want a house that is uniquely theirs—and thus are willing to embark on the sometimes rocky but almost always rewarding road of finding an architect whose work they admire, then working with that architect to find the right site, and developing with the architect the design for a house that is in every important respect an expression of their family and the way they want to live.

Many architects, of course, share these dreams of a uniquely personal house. And they share the same problems as anyone else—for the architect, in confronting the design of his or her own house, has no more of a free rein than anyone else. Like anyone else, they have budget problems. There may be intra-family disagreements over just what the house should be like (and imagine the discussions in families where both husband and wife are architects!). The architect comes at a house-design problem with more options and ideas (trained by education or experience) than most families have ever dreamed of—and thus has more decisions to make. And any architect's house will probably—fairly or not—be looked on as an important expression of his or her talent and skill not just by the neighbors, but by peers and competitors.

In any event, houses designed by architects for themselves have a special interest for anyone interested in studying and understanding good houses. In this book—a totally new second edition of the popular *Houses Architects Design for Themselves* published in 1974—the houses have been organized in chapters to illustrate a variety of options anyone should consider in thinking about their own house:
   • the roots of contemporary design, and learning to understand why contemporary houses are designed the way they are;

• the choices between small and close-in lots and larger suburban lots—and the way those differences in site affect the design of house;

• the special problems (and special pleasures) of vacation houses—and the lessons those informal and relaxed houses suggest about the design of our year-round houses;

• an examination of the special problems of houses designed for hot climates, and the lessons those houses teach about shading and cross-ventilation that are applicable to any house built anywhere it sometimes gets too darn hot—which is almost everywhere; and . . .

• the special techniques used in houses designed to take advantage of solar energy—houses that are not only cheaper to operate, but give their owners the special feeling that they are contributing to a whole new energy-efficient way of living.

Finally, there is also—a first in this new edition—a chapter on apartments architects designed for themselves—designs that create the same kind of very special, very personal way of living offered by custom houses within the considerable constraints of an existing apartment building.

An important note repeated from the first book for those readers who are considering a new house: You will inevitably look first through this book to see if there are any houses that "are just what we're looking for." Chances are you won't find one. You'll find some houses you like, to be sure—that suit your ideas of room arrangement, your ideas of what a house "should look like"—whether that is warmly conservative or starkly modern. But you almost surely will not find one that is just what you are looking for—because the house was not designed with you in mind. It was designed by an architect for his own family—and they do not have the same ideas about their way of living you have about your way of living.

The important use of this book is to help you search for ideas, for forms, for room arrangements, for finishes, for detailing, for ways of fitting a house to its site that please you. What these skilled architects have done for their families will have lessons for you and your family. Try to understand what you like about their houses—and why. Then find yourself a good architect. Together, find a good site, and build a house that pleases you. Then live, as they say, happily ever after.—*Walter F. Wagner Jr.*

Crites House, page 104, Julius Shulman photo.

Vignelli Apartment, page 134,
Norman McGrath photo.

Vedensky House, page 96,
Gerald Lee photo.

Mah House, page 82,
Nick Wheeler photo.

Behn House,
page 54,
Douglas Symes photo.

Platner House, page 25, Ezra Stoller © ESTO photo.

Jacobson House, page 36,
Hugh Stratford photo.

Chapell House, page 76,
Bernard Askienazy photo.

Penney House, page 34, Gordon Schenck photo.

Riley House, page 12,
Norman McGrath photo.

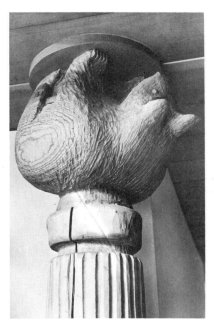

Hoppenfeld House, page 46,
Glen Allison photos.

Osmon House, page 111,
Joshua Freiwald photo.

Buchsbaum Loft,
page 124,
Norman McGrath photo.

Simmons House, page 50,
Robert Lautman photo.

Franzen House, page 102,
David Franzen © ESTO photo.

Lindstrom House, page 14,
Christian Staub photo.

Yaw House, page 142,
David Marlow photo.

Gray House, page 72, Charles White photos.

Hobbs House, page 40,
Art Hupy photo.

1

Where does the design of contemporary houses come from?

There are always roots...

The shape and form of traditional houses are, of course, familiar to almost everyone. On the East Coast, we are familiar with (and comfortable with) the steeply pitched roof, the small-paned windows, the narrow clapboards or shingles, the massive chimneys of the early farmhouses. This familiar design evolved for sensible and understandable reasons. The roof was steeply pitched to shed the snow and run the water off quickly as the snow melted. The windows were small because most of the time in New England it is cold outside; the window panes are small because when those houses were built that was about as big a piece of glass as the local craftsman could make. The clapboards were narrow because that's about the size most pine and fir trees come in. And the chimneys were massive because someone found out pretty early in the game that when a big chimney gets good and warm it continues to give out heat all night long, even after the fire has died down.

The arcades and grand porches of the early Southern houses were there, no surprise, to create shade; and the patio houses of California are built that way for the same reason they have been built in hot European countries for centuries—they create splendid cross ventilation.

Well, the regional rules of nature and weather still apply, and if the limitations imposed by materials are different today—given the huge pieces of glass and the sheets of plywood and the metal sidings and the many forms of masonry and the insulated metal chimneys and the other results of today's technology—materials still shape our design.

And those rules—dictated by region and materials—still shape the design of almost every house, including the very contemporary houses in this book. If many of these houses don't look "familiar," it is because the rules have been interpreted in fresh ways by the architects. And learning to "see" the familiar, the logic, the sources of these houses is learning to be comfortable with contemporary design.

Take the Riley house on the next pages. It is in New England, and it looks like it. It would not be a successful house in Florida, or Texas, or California. At first glance, it looks like a 200-year-old traditional house with its red-stained clapboards, paneled front door, small pane windows, dormers, and steeply pitched roof...but wait. The dormers aren't in the "right place"...they're stacked one above the other. The big central "chimney" isn't a chimney. That formal front door opens...to a greenhouse. And you walk through the greenhouse into...a three-story high central space with...small paned windows on the *inside* wall opening to the upstairs bedrooms but great sliding glass windows letting in the southern sun. As architect Jefferson Riley said: "This house...makes numerous allusions to colonial houses indigenous to its New England context. Yet we did not reproduce these traits by rote, but found joy in assembling them into a unique composition with contemporary strivings of its own."

Or take the Lindstrom house on page 14. This is an extraordinary house—so contemporary in spirit and design that it won a national Honor Award from the American Institute of Architects. It is a house within a house—it can be seen as a flat-roofed house with a roof deck, all covered by an almost free-floating roof of (new materials) translucent fiberglass that creates a unique quality of light in the rooms below. Contemporary? And how. Yet as the article makes clear: "While there is some design influence from the Northwest American Indians seen in the use of massive timber poles and the cross-bracing at the apex of the gable, the Oriental influence is over-powering." Where does the design of contemporary houses come from? There are always roots....

Similarly, architect William Cannady's ranch house (page 18) in Round Top, Texas has such clear roots in "The Wild West" that one almost can see the good guys in the auto court out front and the bad guys on the roof—yet this is a fresh contemporary house designed to be a cool (cross-ventilated) shelter from the hot Texas sun. The design of Peter Woerner's house overlooking a marsh on Long Island Sound grows from very different (and almost literal) roots. Its strong roof form (see page 22) is "envisioned as springing from, and then returning to, the earth in a pure form—an easy and effortless arc."

The final house in this chapter—architect Warren Platner's house in Connecticut (page 25)—returns us to more familiar ground. Here the "familiar" is the materials—cedar shingles, and fieldstone which recall the traditional ways of building in New England. There is also a suggestion of the "house plus additions" sprawl that marks so many New England houses. Roots. But in fact the house is a far cry from any New England farmhouse composition. The procession from drive to auto court to entry and through the house and to the terraces is precise and formal, the outdoor terraces and overlooks are clearly defined by careful landscape design. The house is understood—once you are inside—as a series of pavilions. Thus the house is a progression of pleasant surprises; all reinforced by the meticulous attention to detail and finishing that marks all of Platner's work. And thus, this "familiar-looking house" is one of the most contemporary houses of all....

THE RILEY HOUSE

For this evergreen, stone-chocked New England site, architect Jefferson Riley designed his own house using traditional materials and time-honored building techniques. It is a tall house (four stories including basement) and it rises in a complex profile of setback and projection in each elevation. Dormers protrude from the steeply pitched roof, adding to this sense of complication, and all exterior surfaces are richly mottled with shadow.

The south-facing gable end of the house is opened generously to the sun. The greenhouse below and the varied openings above fill the tall space behind with natural light and warmth. Surplus solar heat collected in the greenhouse is circulated along the insulated foundation wall and stored for radiation at night. The second and third floor bedrooms are set back from the exterior wall but open through windows to the tall space, thus taking advantage of light and view without additional heat loss. Supplementary heating is provided by wood stoves in the kitchen and living room. These stoves vent through the roof and the tall flues accent the verticality of the design.

The volumetric liveliness of the Riley house comes from the interplay of intimate spaces with the unexpectedly tall central space and additional fun is provided by unlooked-for details for double-hung windows on interior walls or a panelled wood door leading to the greenhouse.

Of his non-mainstream approach to design Riley says: "The house with its long gable roof, its double-hung windows, its red-stained clapboards, its central chimney, its over-all bilateral symmetry offset by asymmetrical parts, makes numerous allusions to colonial houses indigenous to its New England context. Yet we did not reproduce these traits by rote, but found joy in assembling them into a unique composition with contemporary strivings of its own."

Architect: Jefferson Riley
  Moore, Grover, Harper
  Essex, Connecticut
Contractor: Essex Builders
Photographer: Norman McGrath

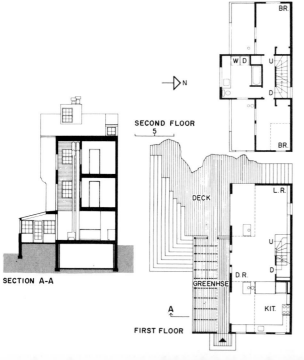

SECTION A-A

SECOND FLOOR
5

N

BR.

W D U

D

BR.

DECK

L.R.

U

D

GREENHSE

D.R.

KIT.

A

FIRST FLOOR

THE MORGAN/LINDSTROM HOUSE

The high quality design of this unique contemporary residence lies with the coalescence of forms and materials. The site is on Bainbridge Island, one of the largest islands in Puget Sound off Seattle; it is heavily wooded with some views to the waterfront. The house was set between two large stands of trees to maximize its isolation from nearby traffic and to permit sunlight to directly hit the entire house. As a bonus, an open children's play yard was created, and it, too, is filled with sunlight.

Called a "structure within a structure" by the architects, an all wood frame supports a superimposed roof, under which is shielded enclosed living quarters. The frame is composed of 24 heavy timber posts and four main beams; a large 7,000-square-foot roof is totally covered with translucent fiberglass roof panels. The integrated "understructure," clad in cedar siding, has a pristine appearance and sharp outline that accentuates the visual strength of horizontal and vertical lines.

The design of the super structure is primarily for visual effect—as the sunlight strikes it, the entire roof lights up, for the translucent roof panels diffuse the sunlight, giving the appearance of a very light and airy structure.

While there is some design influence from structures built by the Northwest American Indians seen in the use of massive timber poles and the cross-bracing at the apex of the gable, an Oriental influence is overpowering. An external spatial sequence exists, from open area, to white-colored rock bordering the pavilion-like building, to an elevated deck, to the great roof. Details of the deck walkway (top right) and the main entrance (bottom right) demonstrate the almost ceremonial procession into the interiors.

Architects: Morgan and Lindstrom
267 Shannon Drive S.E.
Bainbridge Island, Washington
Owner: Mr. & Mrs. R.D. Lindstrom
Contractor: Walt Johnsen Construction
Photographer: Christian Staub

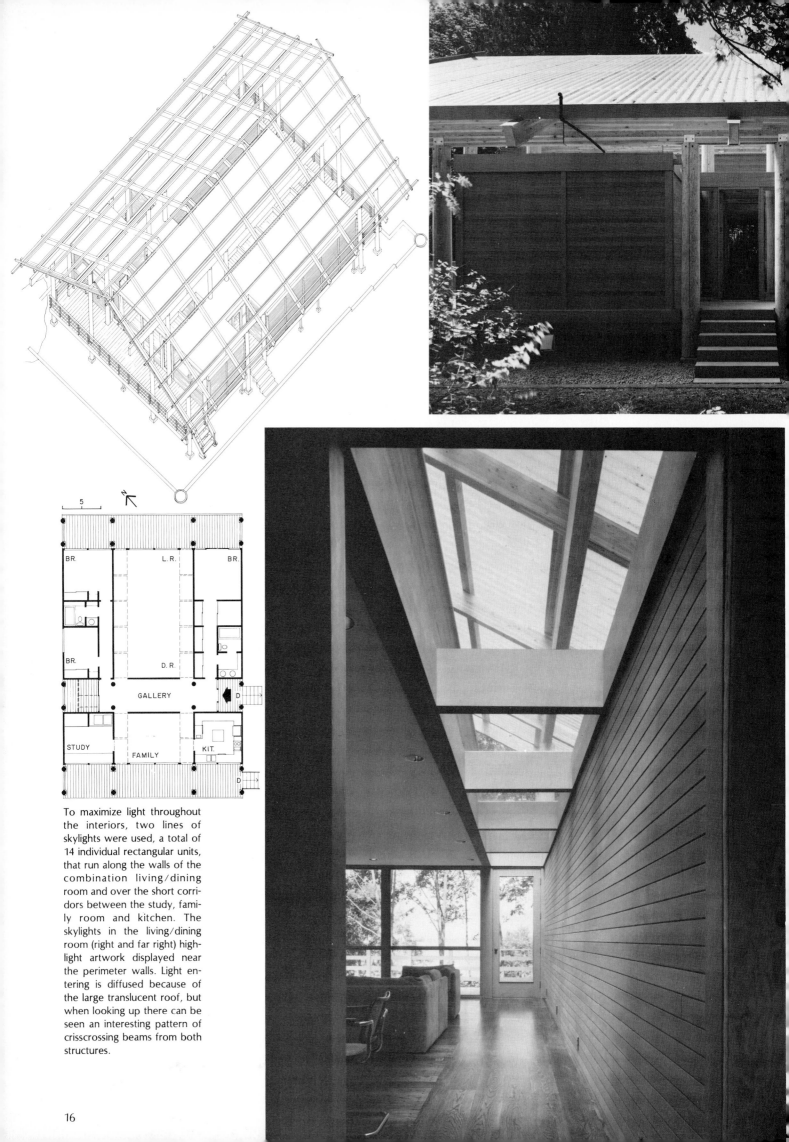

To maximize light throughout the interiors, two lines of skylights were used, a total of 14 individual rectangular units, that run along the walls of the combination living/dining room and over the short corridors between the study, family room and kitchen. The skylights in the living/dining room (right and far right) highlight artwork displayed near the perimeter walls. Light entering is diffused because of the large translucent roof, but when looking up there can be seen an interesting pattern of crisscrossing beams from both structures.

16

On two sides of the house, there is an open veranda. The main entrance (left) is not, however, positioned off the front deck but rather on the side, connecting to a broad interior gallery, off which all rooms flow. Unifying the interiors with the identical exterior material, cedar paneling was specified and timber posts were exposed to tie-in the superstructure as well as continue a processional pattern of spaces established outside. Views to the woods are available from the kitchen (right), family, study and laundry rooms; views to the waterfront are from bedrooms and living/dining area (below).

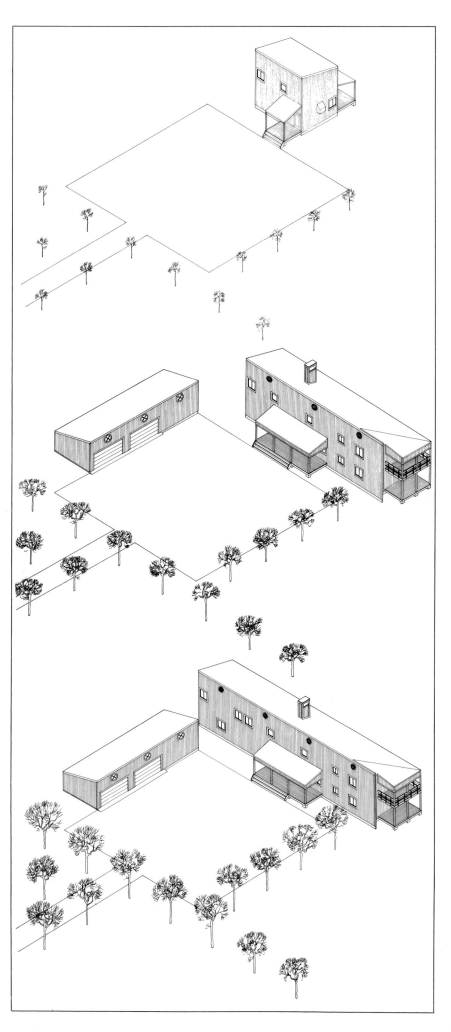

THE CANNADY HOUSE

Destined to become, in the final phase of three-phase development plan, a permane working ranch, this weekend house on t rolling plains of central Texas announces future function in a visual dialect so broad invites a grin. But the architect-owner's o spoken use of the vernacular of the ru Southwest—outbuildings and verand rough wood framing and tin roofs—is te pered by more sophisticated reference establishing through a series of metaph and contrasting statements a controlled d

ue on the architecture of country living.

With its shed-like form and a planar ade that reads almost as an Old West false nt, the house suggests an organic function-m that is belied by its formal siting. Front-on a large auto forecourt, the main build-is flanked on the west by a garage that eats in small its shed configuration and on east by a row of trees to frame a special w. As yet only sketched by saplings nted in the first development phase, the sure of the forecourt will, as the trees

mature, be completed by additional landscaping and a formal drive on the south, boxing a composed square both oasis and landmark in the ranch's largely treeless setting.

To gain cross ventilation from strong prevailing southern winds and capitalize on views across the valley sloping to the north, the house is oriented east – west. Outlined by conventional stud framing and 20-foot clear span timber beams and trusses, its long rectangular plan is staunchly symmetrical, centering on a two-story living-dining space divided

by a freestanding double-sided fireplace whose bulk also hints at an entry hall.

Flanking this common area and separated from it by stairs and service cores are more private quarters: master bedroom and guest suites opening to stacked verandas on the east; kitchen and family room and children's bedrooms (now truncated to kitchenette and bunkroom) on the west.

This studied symmetry of plan, however, is denied in elevations pierced by small square windows whose random rhythm is

The Cannady ranch speaks clearly of its place—expanse of land, constraints of climate and local resource—through simple forms and homespun materials assembled with respectful skill. The weathered exteriors, though rough in finish, are cleanly framed by exposed structural members and carefully detailed, modulating on the interior to smooth stained pine paneling and crisp trim. The effect over-all is one of warmth and welcome expressed with the natural dignity of a dwelling indigenous but not ingenuous.

counterpointed by the regular spacing of attic ventilators. With the added accent of deep offset porches, the fenestration of the house, like its siting, sets up a play of contradiction between plan and volume that sounds in this unpretentious but thoughtfully made ranch-stead a unifying note.

Owner: *William Cannady.* Architects: *Wm. T. Cannady & Associates Inc.* Structural engineer: *Nat Krahl.* Contractor: *Kermit Wunderlich.* Photographer: *Paul Hester*

THE WOERNER HOUSE

"To me, the marsh is a microcosm of life itself, constantly in a state of flux, never static, changing with the seasons, the days, with the tides, with the constant procession of wildlife—ducks, herons, hawks, shorebirds all feeding on what the tide brings in or, in ebbing, uncovers. . . ." Thus architect/owner Peter Woerner de-

scribes his view—a 90-acre tidal marsh facing Long Island Sound. The actual site is a long granite ridge at the edge of the marsh, a ridge that steps down to the eastward suggesting a natural series of half levels. Here, behind a scrim of hickory and oak, Woerner sited his house, a house he envisioned as springing from, and then returning to, the earth in a pure form— an easy and effortless arc.

On the uppermost level, under the arching roof form, the owner has a master bedroom, dressing room, bath and private deck overlooking the marsh. The

level below is given over to guest bedrooms and a studio that are separated by half a level. The lowest levels are kitchen, dining and living spaces, the dining space being framed in greenhouse sections (photo opposite) and opening to a southern exposure. The architect reports that the greenhouse provides a passive solar heating situation with the brick floor over the ledge serving as a heat sink. The living room, drawn back from the glass wall, is sheltering and intimate.

The main perimeter arches were laminated from 2 by 12

planks of Douglas fir with a ½-inch thickness of plywood sandwiched in between. All joints are scarfed and staggered. Joists span between the arches and the whole structure is covered with ½-inch thickness of plywood which acts as a vast stressed skin.

Architect, engineer, owner, contractor:
  Peter Kurt Woerner
  182 Leetes Island Road
  Guilford, Connecticut
Location: Guilford, Connecticut
Graphics consultant: Christina Beebe
Photographer: Robert Perron

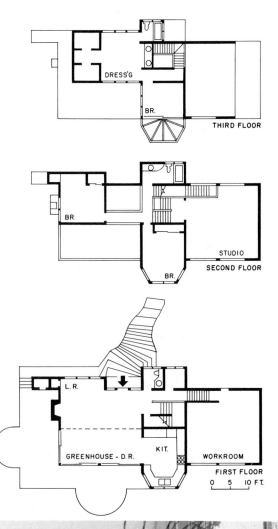

THIRD FLOOR

DRESS'G

BR.

SECOND FLOOR

BR.

STUDIO

BR.

FIRST FLOOR

L. R.

GREENHOUSE - D.R.

KIT.

WORKROOM

0 5 10 FT.

All the principal spaces in the Woerner house open through large expanses of glass to views of the marsh. The studio, photo above, is glazed using a standard industrial sash cut at its edges to fit the curvature of the roof. The plans show a simple, compact, well organized space.

THE PLATNER HOUSE

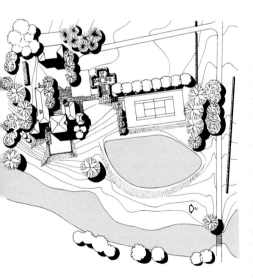

The 2.7-acre site for Warren Platner's own house (plan left) is bounded on the north side by a country road from which a driveway leads to a parking area behind the house in the southeastern part of the property. Here the land falls away sharply to a stream and, beyond, to woods and a salt marsh. "The best buildings," Platner has said, "are conceived as one with the development of the site, and as an extension of and enhancement to their surroundings." In this case the simultaneous development of building and land involved placing the house where it could at once command the most pleasing views and also be screened from the road and entrance drive, providing the occupants and their visitors an appropriate progression from public to private realms. That the house is built on steeply sloping land also provides the chance for a variety of level changes from one part to the next, and the excitement of, for instance, entering the screen porch (extreme left in photograph above) from the terrace on one side and then finding oneself far above the ground on the other.

The roofs and most of the exterior walls of Platner's house are sheathed in white cedar shingles, and the chimney and the screen porch are built of natural fieldstone set in mortar, with the mortar set back and chinking stones used to simulate a dry-set, rubble pattern. These materials, as well as the apparently casual composition of the whole house, help make it—to use the architect's own terms again—an extension and enhancement of the rural surroundings. In an altogether different dimension, the shingles and fieldstone recall traditional ways of building in New England. Though it is, in fact, designed and detailed with great care, the house from the outside exhibits an admirable modesty and respect for the land it occupies.

Ezra Stoller © ESTO photos

Platner conceived his house as a set of separate but interrelated pavilions which vary in scale and outlook as well as in function. The pavilions are arranged loosely, as much in accordance with the qualities of the site as with any compact, formal scheme. Some architects might regard this way of composing a house as too casual, yet the fact remains that it is a way honored by tradition, particularly in farm buildings in New England. The answer to whether it is "good" or "bad" depends to some extent on personal taste. Platner points out that he and his family prefer to live in "a series of separate spaces where each occasion can have its special character," and that the arrangement of his house provides certain other advantages as well. The connections between pavilions, for instance, provide the chance for vertical as well as horizontal movement—down some stairs from the living room to the library, then down

some more to the dining room. The pavilions themselves, too, enclose a terrace on the back of the house, and, on the front and side, they allow for terraces in between—exterior spaces from which to enjoy the pleasures of the site, or descend to the stream or the pond below, the latter of which, together with the tennis court, is another enhancement of the land.

There are a number of bay windows in the house, and many of them have window seats. Spaces that are not actually outdoors, but which do not feel altogether indoors either, they offer still more possibilities for enjoying the landscape. There is indeed an orderly progression from outdoors to in—from the rough, unaltered woodlands and salt marsh to the more carefully manicured lawn on the site itself, to the still more formal terraces, to the bay windows—"inside outsides"—to the interiors of each pavilion. These, as Platner describes them, are

"formal spaces—that is, spaces that visually have definite form—and we live informally in them." They are, too, finished with the meticulous care for which Platner is well known. Each kitchen cabinet, each bookcase, each light fixture, each piece of furniture bears evidence of extensive concern on the part of the designer and considerable craftsmanship on the part of the maker. Together all of these elements, set in the clear and formal spaces of the house, combine to make a true "inside" that stands in sharp and elegant distinction to the Connecticut landscape outdoors.

PLATNER HOUSE, Connecticut. Architects: Warren Platner Associates—associates of Warren Platner on this project: David Connell, Paul Plumer, and James Wiebe. Engineers: Pfisterer, Tor and Associates (structural); John A. Altieri (mechanical/electrical). Consultants: Jill Mitchell (graphics); Sheila Hicks (textiles). Contractor: The George C. Field Company.

Since the house is made up of
five pavillions, four of them
connected (plan below), there
are views across terraces from
one part to another (left and
right). The most frequently used
entrance to the house is through
the kitchen (below), "where", as
Platner points out, "the action
often is." One proceeds through
the library (below right) up five
stairs to the living room (shown
on the following two pages).

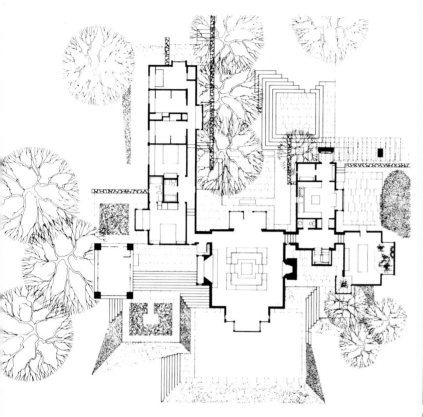

One of the bedrooms is shown on the left; it is small and compact, and its window overlooks a wooded ravine below. The dining room (shown below) is designed to include a conservatory, but in such a way that it is the plants, rather than the people, who are in the sun.

All contemporary design has roots....

Again, learning to "see" the familiar, the logic, the evolutionary character of these contemporary houses is learning to be comfortable with contemporary design.

Each of these houses—designed by architects for their own families—is very different. Each reflects a different kind of site, a different climate, different family needs, different ideas of ways of living, different personal preferences.

But each—like all of the houses that follow, houses for the city, for the suburbs, for vacation use—has roots. Each has grown from the land, from its materials, from regional traditions....

2

In houses for small and close-in lots, outdoor living and privacy must be designed in...

The "architects' own houses" shown in the first chapter of this book are—like many custom houses—on large and sometimes isolated sites. But many architects and their families—like many of us—either need or wish to live in or close to the city. For some, job schedules make a long commute unacceptable. Other families want no part of the quiet or isolation of the countryside and want to be close to the schools, or close to playmates for the children, or "close to everything."

Typically, the lots for these "close-in" houses are small, and that presents problems—the kind of problems that offer design opportunities to an architect and very special benefits to owners. For example:

The typical built-for-sale house on a small lot offers relatively little privacy. Large lots create privacy simply because they are big; on small lots privacy has to be "created" or "designed in"—by placement of the house on the lot in relation to neighbors and existing plantings or site contour; by organization of rooms within the house; by artful placement (or deliberate elimination) of windows; by new fences or screens or trellises.

Outdoor living space in most builder subdivisions just happens, for typically there are not-very-usable front yards marked off at regular intervals by driveways with cars parked on them; useless side yards across which windows of neighboring houses stare at each other; and backyard patios overlooking the patios of both neighboring houses and the patio of the house on the next street. Each of the nine houses in this chapter has truly usable (and in most cases, truly private) outdoor living—though these houses are on narrow lots with, in most cases, neighbors right alongside.

And further, you will find in each of these nine houses architects designed for their own families all of the characteristics that separate good custom design from most built-for-sale housing. These houses too have "roots"—in tradition, in materials, in form. Specifically, the house by architect Thompson Penney on the next pages interprets in contemporary and modest-budget terms "the physical and philosophical characteristics of the 18th- and 19th-century Charleston houses." This house would fit into a streetscape of 150-year-old houses; and it does fit the life style of the family that built it. Another house sensitively related to an established neighborhood, but also sited and shaped to take advantage of a long-range view of lake and mountains, is the Jacobson house on pages 36-39. And the house is designed to create outdoor privacy both on the street side and in back.

Three of the houses—the Hobbs house (page 40), the Williams house (page 42), and the Behn house (page 54)—show how effectively good architects can use steep sites—the kind of "unbuildable" land that is often by-passed by builders and the timid custom-house client. In the Hobbs house, rooms on four levels have big windows overlooking the view, and two striking decks on the southern exposure create outdoor living at treetop level. In the Williams house, private outdoor terraces are defined and given privacy (though they are only feet from the street) by the slope and the way it is terraced. The Behn house is a "tight little ship"—a 28-foot-square shape almost totally closed to the road and the neighboring houses in a dense Berkeley, California neighborhood—but open with decks on both living levels to breathtaking views over the Golden Gate.

The Cannady house (page 44) shows an exceedingly interesting arrangement of house on site to make the most of limited outdoor area: the house is set to the rear of the lot (with parking under, off a rear alley) to create one big outdoor area—and the architect also developed a totally private "tree-house" roof terrace. The Hoppenfeld house (page 46) in Albuquerque, New Mexico develops almost every square inch of the small, flat, and arid site—and even provides for the family a most unusual and quite beautiful pond view. Tasso Katselas' house for his family on a downtown Pittsburgh lot makes very effective use of a sloping site—the spaces of the house are on a series of platforms—"a house of almost unbroken vertical flow, a design with enormous visual energy and dynamism." (See page 58.) To see just how much varied space an architect can fit into a narrow city lot, see Thomas Simmons' handsome project in the Georgetown area of Washington, D.C. (page 50). In two phases, he fit onto the lot his own house, two rental units, and his small architectural office—all sharing a backyard pool and planting area.

One final and very special kind of design for tight urban sites is the Menashe cottage in Berkeley. This tiny building—a garage and guest house for a larger residence further up the steep site—was designed to replace a Maybeck-inspired cottage that burned. Thus this little composition, beautifully hand-crafted, was designed not in an attempt to literally reproduce the original (since that would have been virtually impossible), but to reproduce the spirit of the original and thus be in harmony and sympathy with the remaining older house. This is a very difficult piece of contextual design—very well carried out.

THE PENNEY HOUSE

The architect of this house reports that his goal was not to create a "caricature" of traditional Charleston architecture (photo left) by mimicking its details, but instead to seek "the physical and philosophical characteristics of the eighteenth- and nineteenth-century Charleston single house which are valid in our own time, and to interpret these in a contemporary building." Built in a suburb near Charleston designated by its developer as a version of the traditional Charleston neighborhood, the house turns its short side to the street, and on the south it opens onto a side yard. The old-fashioned two-story piazza, or porch, is here left unroofed, and it is interrupted by a stair tower which moved outwards to make room for the un-traditional kitchen which was inserted inside.

PENNEY HOUSE, Mount Pleasant, South Carolina. Architect: *Thompson E. Penney.* General contractor: *Baker-Hunt Construction Co.*

SECOND FLOOR

FIRST FLOOR

THE JACOBSON HOUSE

Building a new house in an old neighborhood poses special problems of compatibility with nearby existing houses and at the same time, the problems of obtaining the kind of character and amenity that the owners of the new house want for themselves. In this Seattle house, built in an established neighborhood of fairly high density, architect Philip Jacobson has provided for himself and his family a contemporary house suited to their needs and making the most of the site, without doing violence to the form and character of the area. The new house adopts the pitched roof of surrounding houses but uses it in a highly individual way, achieving a sense of simplicity in its long, low uncomplicated line. The palette of materials used on the exterior is small: all-white stucco to give continuity and, again, simplicity to the exterior forms, and asphalt shingles on the roof for the same basic reasons. Inside, the same careful use of a few materials minimizes the visual complexity of the non-rectilinear, varied spaces organized around a central stairway. The off-white walls allow for display of art and for strong color accents in wall hangings, area rugs and furniture. Elegant detailing—in window and door jambs, sills, wall bases, book shelves, fireplace, alcoves for art, and in the sauna and its skylight— are handled with such simplicity that they in no way distract from the basic simplicity of the interior with its variety of spaces—from large, high and open, to small, intimate and enclosed. As much natural light as possible is admitted, both directly and indirectly, to minimize the darkness of winter days. For bright days, wood slat roller blinds on windows and an exterior vinyl roller awning on the skylight protect from solar radiation. All artificial light is indirect.

Since the site has a fine view of Lake Washington, Mount Rainier and the Cascade Mountains, the living room opens toward this view, and its deck, like that of the master bedroom, acts as an extension of the room toward a private landscaped area.

Form, line, color and texture are handled with great simplicity to achieve continuity from exterior to interior, and to allow for a contemporary expression of the owners' wishes and needs.

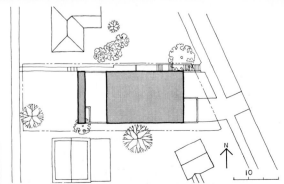

Architect: Philip L. Jacobson
    3935 51st N.E.
    Seattle, Washington
Owners: Mr. and Mrs. Philip L. Jacobson
Location: Seattle, Washington
Contractor: Tom Paulsell Construction Co.
Photographers: Hugh Stratford;
    Philip Jacobson

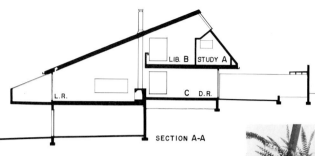

SECTION A-A

A

The spaces of the house are varied in form as in size, deriving interest from their location under the roof which is expressed on the interior more than usual. The long slope of the cedar plank ceiling and off-white walls of the living room (opposite page) make it the most dramatic interior space, but small enclosed spaces such as those shown above and at right have individuality of a different kind. Brick pavers in the dining room (below) are a visual continuance of the brick paths outside. Natural light fills the balcony which overhangs the living room and, along with the vertical line of the fireplace flues, emphasizes the volume of this room.

B

C

THE HOBBS HOUSE

A steep, urban site sloping to the east with a view of woods, Lake Washington and the Cascade Mountain Range in the distance. Space for functions both common and private for two parents and three children. Architect Richard Hobbs brought these givens together in a l6-foot by 46-foot rectangular plan that distributes its functions over six interior levels. The entry level leads down to the children's areas or up to the main spaces of the house. Off these main spaces, and facing the view, is a narrow greenhouse that provides—in addition to a profusion of house plants—a fine sense of openness to the deck and woods beyond (photo below right).

Only from the downhill side does the verticality of the scheme reveal itself completely. From this vantage, the elaborately sculpted wood forms reach right to the tree tops giving the occupants of the upper levels a remarkable sense of privacy and an exhilarating feeling of elevation.

The interiors are carefully worked out and considerable spatial interest is achieved by powerful diagonal forms and by graceful circular projections into the main spaces. The extraordinary variety of openings also enriches the spaces, filling the interiors with daylight and broad streaks of sun that are especially welcome in the Northwest.

Heating is provided by a four zone system employing both electric baseboard and forced air units controlled from a central location. The principal finishes are cedar siding, anodized aluminum window frames, and gypsum board on ceilings and interior walls.

Architects: Hobbs Fukui
    150l Belmont Avenue
    Seattle, Washington
Owner: Richard Hobbs
Engineers:
    Robert G. Albrecht (structural)
    Neil H. Twelker (foundations)
    Martin/Datacom Associates (mechanical)
Interiors: Dallas E. Zeiger
Landscape: Thomas L. Berger
Contractor: Stole Building Co.
Photographer: Art Hupy

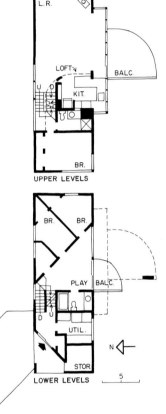

UPPER LEVELS

LOWER LEVELS

L.R.

LOFT   BALC.

KIT.

BR.

BR.   BR.

PLAY   BALC.

UTIL.

STOR.

N

5

Materials familiar to Seattle—the cedar siding and lath—are here used in unfamiliar ways. The strong horizontal planes of the garage wall, the stairs to the terrace, the living room and, behind it, the main body of the house are strikingly set off by the rounded shapes of the lattice. . . .

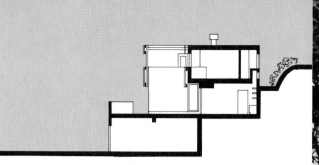

THE WILLIAMS HOUSE

This strong and handsome house was shaped by an extraordinary set of constraints: The lot is steep, only 50 by 120 feet, with 10-foot setback requirements front and back, and a height limitation to protect the view of the house up the hill. The design had to side-step an existing garage which, under city ordinance, could not have living space above it. Finally, the view is to the south and southwest—and thus into the sun.

And thus the lacework of lath that shades the windows from the high summer sun without blocking the view or the sparse sunlight of Seattle's long gray winters.

The rounded forms of this dominant design element are a striking foil to the strong flat planes of the house, and are echoed softly inside the house (see plan). And in time, the lath will be a trellis of vines and plants—a gesture to the neighborhood of "returning" the site toward its original condition—a landscaped garden.

Despite the initial impression of complexity, the house is quite simple in form and plan. Photos right show the two main living spaces: The living room, given extra height by being set four steps down the hillside; and the two-story-high kitchen/dining space, center of activity for the Williams and their two boys. Both share the view and open to the terrace and gardens. The lower floor also has architect Williams' studio and a more formal dining space; a curving stair (echoing the forms outside) leads up to the bedroom level. The master bedroom extends out over the living room and has its own screened outdoor deck.

This is a splendid urban house.

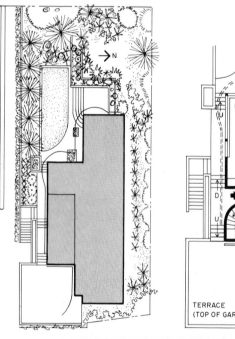

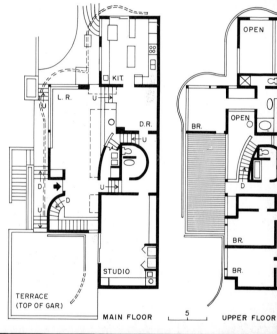

MAIN FLOOR   5   UPPER FLOOR

Architect and owner: Gerald A. Williams of TRA,
    4720 N. E. 36th Street
    Seattle, Washington
Engineers: Donald G. Radcliffe of TRA
    (structural), Robert D. Wells (mechanical)
Interior design consultant: William Wright
    of TRA with the architect
Landscape architect: Dorothy Hussey
Contractor: Tom Paulsen
Photographer: Michael Burns

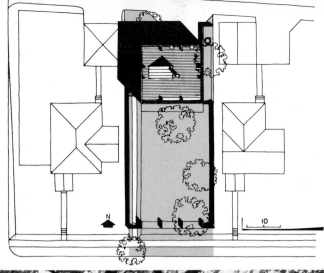

Jonathan King

THE CANNADY HOUSE

In designing a house for his own family of four, in a Houston subdivision, architect William Cannady began with two important design decisions. First, he set the house at the rear of the lot creating in this way one large outdoor area instead of two smaller areas and avoiding the standard shoulder-to-shoulder relationship with neighbors. Second, he placed the house over the garage and developed an inviting roof terrace that provided a second usable outdoor space—this one to be used primarily by parents for cocktails and cookouts. The six-

foot side yard restrictions and the pattern of existing trees combined to determine the precise siting as well as the 33- by 37-foot outside dimensions.

Kitchen, study, dining and living room, share the second floor and flow easily around a sharply defined central core. The level above is compartmentalized into parents' and children's bedrooms and baths. The floor of the master bedroom is cut back to create a narrow vertical connection with the living room below (section and photo, opposite page).

The structure is standard wood frame, clad inside and out with 1- by 6-inch rough sawn cedar siding. Painted sheetrock is used selectively on ceilings and third floor partitions. The floor of the living room level is finished in clay tile imported from Mexico and the roof terrace is 1- by 4-inch redwood decking constructed in pallets.

According to Cannady, a very low cost was achieved for several reasons. The quantity and cost of finish materials was not excessive. But beyond that, almost no unusual detailing con-

ditions were allowed to creep into the drawings and the contractor understood, and was sympathetic to, the architect/owners's rather straightforward design intention from the outset.

Architect and *owner:* WILLIAM T. CANNADY. *Location:* Houston, Texas. *Engineers:* Krahl & Gaddy (structural). *Landscape architect:* Carlisle Becker. *Contractor:* Design Fabricators, Gene Hopkins, partner-in-charge.

The creation of a rooftop terrace brought the useable outdoor coverage to virtually 100 per cent of the site—an objective that seems especially sensible for a small lot in a warm climate. Projecting vents are carefully located to intrude as little as possible (photo left). A solid parapet and surrounding trees help to preserve a pleasant sense of privacy when the roof deck is in use.

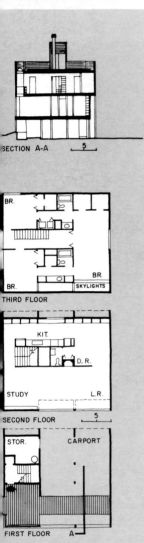

SECTION A-A   5

THIRD FLOOR

BR.

BR.   BR.
                SKYLIGHTS

SECOND FLOOR   5

KIT.

D.R.

STUDY   L.R.

FIRST FLOOR   A

STOR.   CARPORT

Photos by Richard Payne except as noted

Although there is a gas-fired warm air system used as a backup, passive techniques keep the house comfortable most of the year. Two exhaust fans and an evaporative cooler help to maintain summer comfort and two roof-mounted solar panels supply domestic hot water year around. The corrugated metal roofing serves to reflect the sun and, like the stucco-covered adobe block, is characteristic of the region.

THE HOPPENFELD HOUSE

The sheer delight of this Albuquerque house by architect Morton Hoppenfeld is apparent in almost every photo. The house is a small-lot solution to typical problems of privacy where freestanding, six-foot-high adobe walls serve as screens and where every square foot of the site is put to service. The well fed pond, for instance, provides not only an anomalous beauty but serves as a device for moderating the micro-climate in a flat, semiarid district where noondays can be murderously hot but nights cool even in summer.

The south end of the Hoppenfeld house is thrown open like a green house to trap the winter sun and hold its heat in thick masonry floors and walls. To guard against summer overload, these glass sections are covered by a latticework of wood strips that, together with newly-planted cottonwood trees (photo below right) will make a filtered canopy. The rest of the plan, with the exception of the master bath, offers few surprises. Major spaces are pivoted around a kitchen that is clearly a focus of family activity.

What is most extraordinary about the Hoppenfeld house— and the feature that most sharply distinguishes it from others in this group—is the free use the architect has made of unusual, unexpected and sometimes idiosyncratic details (see photos next page). They are more than an assertion of personal values. These column capitals and eccentric bits of ironwork give the design a tactile richness that can be felt in every space and a sense of fun that is pervasive and absolutely beguiling.

HOPPENFELD RESIDENCE, Albuquerque, New Mexico. Architect: *Morton Hoppenfeld*. Construction manager: *Ron Romero*.

Glen Allison photos

Unusual column caps and fixture details (photos right) enrich the already lively interiors. Latticework applied over the greenhouse sections (photos above right) filters the sunlight in summer into the dining space and master bath. Douglas fir and stucco on plaster applied both inside and outside, create strong visual contrasts, contrasts that are heightened by planting and agreeable color accents.

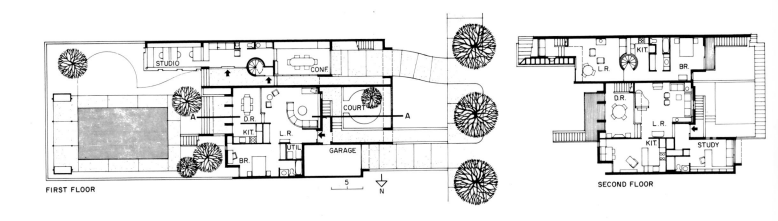

FIRST FLOOR

SECOND FLOOR

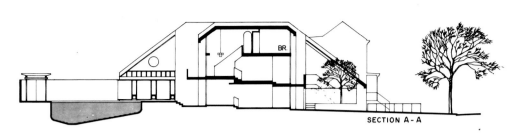

SECTION A-A

Robert Lautman photos

THE SIMMONS HOUSE

A decade ago, architect Thomas B. Simmons purchased a vacant lot in southeast Washington, D.C., and built a townhouse for his family that included in its design a single, lower-floor rental unit. He then went to work in a local firm. When he decided recently to open his own practice, Simmons bought an adjacent lot and made a substantial addition to his earlier house. The new addition includes his office on the ground floor, a new master bedroom above and a second rental unit, this time a small duplex, also over the office.

The architect describes the situation as "a kind of affluent commune with none of the messy, shared privacies so mistakenly undertaken by real communes—each unit has complete separation, just the amenities are shared." These amenities are not inconsiderable. They include a handsome swimming pool and garden for flowers and vegetables, all arranged in the consolidated backyard space (photo right).

The new office space (photo overleaf) faces the pool and is generously north lighted through glass walls that keep the narrow linear volume from feeling constricted. Operable panels admit pleasant summer breezes.

For his new wing, Simmons has freely introduced new forms and details—especially new kinds of openings—but collected them under the same metal roof and integrated them easily into a single, united composition. A lot happens in these volumes but the spaces do not seem tortured and the functions (house, rental apartments, office) are carefully organized to complement each other in a variety of ways.

SIMMONS RESIDENCE AND OFFICE, Washington, D.C. Architect: *Thomas B. Simmons*. Structural engineer for addition: *Carl Hansen*. Landscape architect: *Ferco Goldinger*. Contractor for addition: *architect/owner*.

The dining space (photo left) and the office (photo across page) both focus on the pool and garden at the rear of the property. The new master bedroom (photo below) overlooks the entry court. The narrow conference area (photo right) is an extension of the drafting area that opens through a wheel window to the same entry court.

THE BEHN HOUSE

Architect Peter Behn's house for his own family of four rises from a steeply sloping site in the Berkeley hills, a site with unobstructed views to the west out the Golden Gate. Apart from the parking platform and entry, the street or uphill side of the house is completely closed for privacy and sound separation. On the south and west, the house is considerably more open though even here the decks and window walls can be closed off by two layers of roll-up shades—one inside and one out—a simple device for modulating breezes and controlling glare from a low winter sun.

The plan is a 28-foot square with functions distributed over three levels. The lowest level contains the architect's studio, an isolated space that is linked to the rest of the house only by an external stair. Living room, dining room, kitchen and deck occupy the intermediate level while the upper level is given over to parents' and children's bedrooms. Only the bath and children's bedroom can be closed off completely. All the other volumes, excepting of course the studio, flow into each other rather freely, borrowing space, returning it, establishing spatial definition of various degrees.

The architect describes the eclectic imagery of the house—and particularly certain details—as "nautical." The system of turnbuckles on the deck railings and curtained storage walls throughout are cited as examples. For the rest, he says, he drew on his recollections of Italy where he and his wife lived for several years.

In the selection of conventional framing, however, as well as primary finishes—cedar shingle and boards—the Behn house is a Bay Area solution, and a lively, expressive one.

Architect: Peter Behn
  1709A Delaware Street
  Berkeley, California
Owners: Peter and Kathie Behn
Structural engineer: Raymond Lindahl
Photographer: Douglas Symes

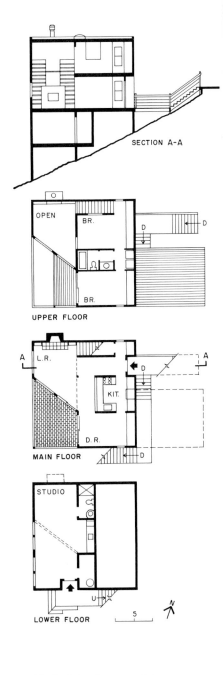

SECTION A-A

OPEN
BR.
D
D
BR.

UPPER FLOOR

L.R.
A
A
D
KIT.
D.R.
D

MAIN FLOOR

STUDIO
U

LOWER FLOOR

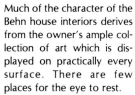

5

N

Much of the character of the Behn house interiors derives from the owner's ample collection of art which is displayed on practically every surface. There are few places for the eye to rest.

THE KATSELAS HOUSE

The sections, more than any other drawings, convey the character of Katselas' own house built on a small piece of property behind a streetfront house in downtown Pittsburgh. To satisfy local code, his house had to physically attach itself to the streetfront house—which it does with a single wood tie—then soar upward in a sequence of superimposed platforms to claim its share of sun and sky. The half-level solution could have produced a static series of semi-isolated spaces. It did not. Instead it produced a house of almost unbroken vertical flow, a design with enormous visual energy and dynamism. To generate the number and variety of spaces required, Katselas developed eight half-levels. Most, of course, derive their individuality from the functions they accomodate, but they are made into a unified whole by the structural grid of concrete columns and wood and concrete girders that frames the entire house. Throughout the design, a complex geometry of triangles, rectangles and circles has been skillfully integrated into this grid. From the uppermost levels of the house, where the need for privacy no longer requires the use of glass block in the openings, pleasant views of the neighborhood begin to emerge.

The stairs are simply detailed in wood and steel and left open to give them a visual prominence appropriate to a scheme of such markedly vertical development. Every space in the house has been tastefully personalized by built-ins, by carefully selected furnishings and, perhaps most especially, by the booty lovingly collected in the course of extensive foreign travel.

KATSELAS RESIDENCE Pittsburgh. Architect: *Tasso Katselas*. Structural engineers: *Gensert, Peller Associates*; Landscape architect: *Joseph Hajnas*; Interior consultant: *Paul Planert*; Contractor: *Sabina Construction*.

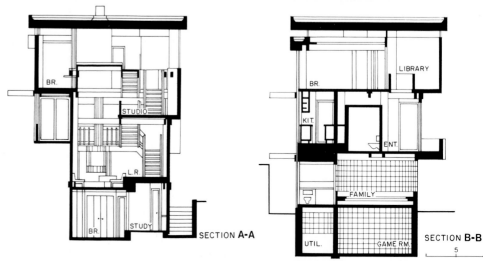

SECTION A-A

SECTION B-B

Nick Wheeler photos

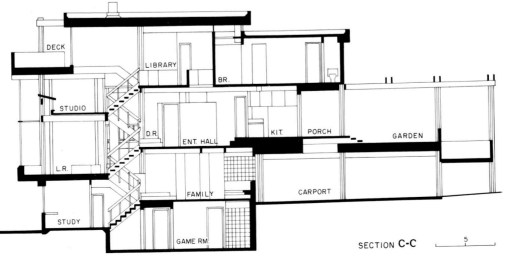

DECK

LIBRARY

BR.

STUDIO

D.R.

ENT. HALL

KIT.

PORCH

GARDEN

L.R.

FAMILY

CARPORT

STUDY

GAME RM.

SECTION **C-C**

The outdoor spaces are developed at front and rear. On the approach side is a raised terrace-garden that is lightly screened for privacy. Behind the house (see photo opening page) is a small pool—"more for cooling off than for swimming" says Katselas. Also visible in that same photo is a Vierendeel truss used as a sheer element to stiffen the frame at the back of the house. The truss also supports the platform over the living room that serves Katselas as a studio.

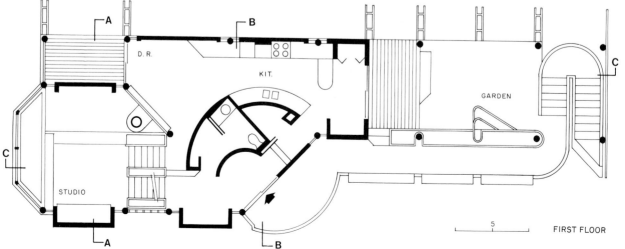

D. R.

KIT.

GARDEN

STUDIO

5

FIRST FLOOR

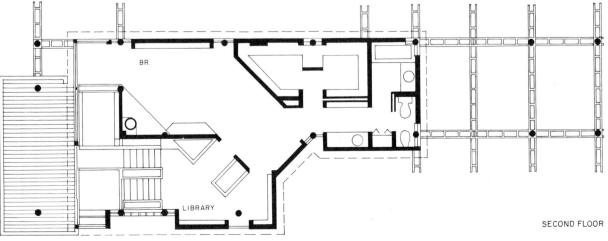

BR.

LIBRARY

SECOND FLOOR

THE MENASHE COTTAGE

"It has often been pointed out that all sound art is an expression springing from the nature which environs it. Its principles may have been imported from afar, but the application of those principles must be native. A home, for example, must be adapted to the climate, the landscape and the life in which it is to serve its part."
From The Simple Home, *by Charles Keeler, dedicated to Bernard Maybeck, 1904.*

Once a building has been destroyed, it can never be re-created—only reproduced. And a reproduction, however faithful, is destined to be but a pale reflection of that which it struggles to emulate. The built landscape is littered with ersatz imitations of Colonial, Tudor, Victorian—easy prey. But the difference between an original and a reproduction is that the former is a specific response to a particular set of circumstances, whereas the latter is merely an appropriation of form.

San Francisco architect Howard Menashe has reconstructed a small guest cottage originally designed by a student of Bernard Maybeck, and last year destroyed by fire. But rather than pull from the ashes a duplicate, Menashe has grafted a sensitive hybrid. His success, perhaps, stems from his intention "to re-create a spiritual likeness of the older cottage by incorporating many of the original spatial and external gestures in the new design . . . but with substantial adjustments."

The cottage was first designed as a reduced likeness of a larger, main house sited directly uphill (see section left), and functions as an ancillary space—either guest house or studio. Its neighborhood is densely built in a historically rich vernacular—it was home for Maybeck and the Hillside Club, a small group of naturalists, poets, and artists, headed by Keeler, responsible for promoting the "Bay Region style" in the early Twenties. The exterior is clad in traditional redwood to blend comfortably with the wooded site; stained dark at street level to meld with the hill, and left natural on the top to lighten and define the living spaces. A terne-coated stainless roof, with a new cupola tower over the rear entry, serves as a visual reference point to distinguish the cottage from the main house. The cupola also functions as a light well, to let sun into the hillside interior spaces. Only the fireplace, garage footings, and garage door were salvaged from the fire; but instead of appearing as historical icons, they have been carefully integrated into their new but sympathetic context.

The nexus between the Maybeck-inspired original and the Menashe reconstruction is perhaps a shared appreciation of natural materials, and a sensitivity to the texture of the landscape.

Randall Fleming photos

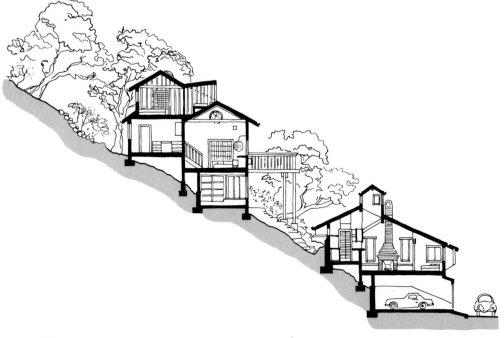

MENASHE COTTAGE, Berkeley, California. Architects: *Howard David Menashe—associate architect: Ann Hughes.* Engineer: *Paul Juilly* (structural). Contractor: *Howard David Menashe.*

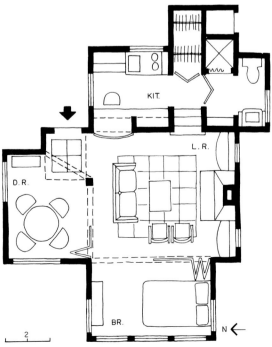

Carol Stout

The cottage features an unusually high standard of craftsmanship. The materials were chosen for their warmth and texture, and have been left unadorned. A massive fireplace serves to focus the open space. A shutter track system, for privacy in the bathroom and sleeping alcove (photo below), is incorporated into a fascia band that coheres the space and unifies the two floor levels. A specially designed and turned fir column gestures toward the light-emitting cupola, and here again, the fascia is worked across to define the dining area and entry.

A final thought about these architect-designed houses on small urban sites...

Each of these houses makes clear the potential of good custom design. These houses are not "spectacular"—they do not compete or shout for attention amidst their more conventional neighbors. But they clearly show the alternative to the plain vanilla lined up by speculative homebuilders on the same kind of streets in the same cities. They show the "something very special" that good architects can offer their clients—as they offered something special to their own families in these carefully designed houses. And that is one of the things that architects do for a living. . . .

3

Given a larger site, some houses are shaped by the land; others *give* shape to a featureless lot

The six houses on the next pages explore another essential root of good contemporary design; relating the house to the site. In the previous chapter on close-in houses, the sites—being small—presented a rigid discipline. In each case the house was shaped by the limited area available, shaped by the need to create privacy with design, and shaped by having to relate esthetically to close-by neighbors. These restrictions are released when a house is to be built on a larger lot. As has been suggested earlier, privacy from neighbors comes with the size of a larger lot, and need not be designed in. The house has less need (though cost remains a factor) for compactness—there is room to sprawl. And of course, away from neighbors, the design of the house can be as free as it wants to be—these houses are objects in and of themselves, with little need to relate esthetically to the neighborhood's familiar forms and traditions. Thus, the major design constraint for houses on larger sites is—while making the house just right for the family that is going to live there—making it suit the site.

The first two houses in this chapter—designed by architects James Caldwell and John Slack for their families—are very much shaped by their sites. The Caldwell house is on a heavily wooded site with a clearing that slopes down to a creek passing by. Everything about the house relates to these conditions: the house is in the clearing for a maximum of sun, the rest of the one-acre site is left natural as a shield against the road and neighbors. The house is shaped so that every room except two bedrooms has a direct view of the creek. There are two very separate outdoor living areas—both decks—one for outdoor entertainment, the other for quiet outdoor dining.

The Slack house (page 70) is perhaps more formal—on a more manicured kind of suburban lot. But again there were site considerations—this time a problem of water run-off through the site, which dictated turning the house at a 45-degree angle to the road to separate the water as it ran down the site to the house. This decision in turn suggested the use of the 45-degree angle inside the house—creating a variety of lively rooms and unexpected spaces. Again, a very handsome and sensitive design growing out of opportunities and/or constraints established by the site.

But what are the opportunities when the site is flat—as most land in this broad country is? How do you create the kind of drama and excitement of a hillside house or a mountainside house or a house with a stunning water view when the land is flat and relatively featureless? You design in the drama and excitement; that is (again) one of the things that architects do for a living, and what the architects of the remaining four houses in the chapter did for their own houses.

The Jaffe house (page 78) exhibits the kind of "roots" discussed in the first chapter—it is fashioned with wood shingles, steep roofs, a big chimney—but on a flat, former-farm field, these characteristics are "drawn-out," perhaps even exaggerated, to make the house a stronger composition—a stronger object dominating a relatively featureless site.

For his family, architect Paul Gray designed a much more formal composition: this house (page 72) is crisp and geometric and precise. It is—appropriately for its site and for the family size—a rather spread-out house. In its wooded site, this house is treated as a rather elegant composition of shapes, joined by hallways and set off by carefully designed and finished outdoor spaces—including a pool that repeats the crisp geometrics of the house. This house is again a strong presence on its site.

The Chapell house also has a kind of design formality as you approach; but inside (as is appropriate for the needs of a very different family) the house is developed in an entirely different way. The interior is treated as one great two-story space (the living room, of course) opening on the south to an equally large outdoor deck. The other rooms, on both levels, are treated as alcoves off this central public space. This is a house not of rooms, but of spaces divided by simple planes of wall; all creating a rather fanciful shape that (once again) creates a strong sculptural object on an essentially featureless piece of land.

The final house in this chapter—architect Francis Mah's house on a suburban street in Memphis—in many ways appears to be the most conventional in the chapter. It is—typical to the area—low lying, with a low hipped roof. On the contrary, it is highly experimental—the kind of house it is appropriate for an architect to design for his own family, taking "risks" he might not ask a client to underwrite. Here, architect Mah has built the conventional rooms of his house around a vast garden room with a translucent roof—a space that is a greenhouse, and a pool enclosure, and an effective collector of solar heat. This makes the house a very private one for a dense suburban area, for the bulk of "outdoor living" takes place in the important indoor space. It is a house full of surprises—and elegant surprises; which is of course one of the things any good architect-designed house should offer its owners....

THE CALDWELL HOUSE

The odd shape of the lot on which this house is built comes from the creek which meanders along one side; and while it made for some challenging problems, it also provided exceptional advantages of which the architect has availed himself. The house is placed in the most open part of the one-acre lot, where it gets both sunlight and a fine view down the creek, and remains secluded and protected from the road by the splendid grove of redwoods which are on the site. The house angles with the curve of the creek, so that almost every room gains by having a view of the creek. Skylights and clerestory windows not only bring in welcome amounts of sunlight but allow for views into the treetops from rooms otherwise without an outlook. The budget for the house was small, especially in relation to the spaces desired. The result, however, belies any sense of restriction, and as the architect says, "There was never a compromise with finish materials: we used cedar shingles on the exterior, and hardwood floors and handmade tile inside." By opening the main rooms to each other, horizontally and vertically, the interior spaces seem larger than they actually are, an effect enhanced by the amount and quality of the natural light which various types of openings admit, and by the relation of interior spaces to the large deck off the living and dining rooms. The plan is unusually compact, and allows for considerable flexibility in use of the house: some of the open areas can be closed off for privacy and quiet, an apartment over the garage and the future addition of an already designed family room are other features of this flexibility.

This orderly framing system is based on a four-foot module, with beams exposed throughout the house. The architect/owner was also contractor and, to keep costs down, did much of the construction himself.

Architect: James E. Caldwell, Jr.
  243 Vallejo Street
  San Francisco, California
Owners: Mr. & Mrs. James E. Caldwell, Jr
Location: Woodside, California
Engineers:
  Shapiro, Okino & Hom (structural)
  George Aronovsky (mechanical)
Interior designer: Philipa Caldwell
Landscape architects: Richard Schardt
  Thomas Church
Contractor: James E. Caldwell, Jr.
Photographer: Philip Molten

SECOND FLOOR

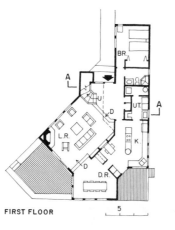

FIRST FLOOR

SECTION A-A

Clerestories, skylights and windows give this house an extraordinarily light and open feeling, and the easy flow of spaces both vertically and horizontally suggests that the house has more than its actual 2100 square feet of space. Without cramping or crowding, the compact plan has no wasted spaces.

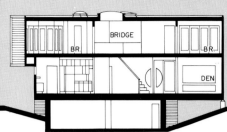

THE SLACK HOUSE

The site fell off sharply from the level of the access road and surface runoff spilled down a ravine through the center of the site. With these challenges in mind, Slack sought and obtained a variance which permitted him to locate the detached garage on an area of high ground that encroached into the required 35-foot setback. This was the key. Then by rotating the foundation wall for the house 45 degrees from the road axis, the water runoff was divided into two channels; one passing harmlessly near the rear of the garage, the other collected into a scupper under the front entry bridge. The remaining upper structure is supported by concrete piers spaced 12 feet on center.

The axis of the road reasserts itself in the enclosed plastic barrel vault that links house with garage and in various sections of exterior wall and interior partition. The result is a lively geometry that produces some unexpected volumes inside. Circulation is confined to a triangular pattern off the entry while the major spaces open to the downhill side to views of the heavily-treed lot. The pattern upstairs is similar except that two of the three bedrooms overlook the double-height living room below. The roof over the upstairs hall is heavily pierced with skylights (photo upper right) that admit daylight through a triangular opening in the floor to the main level below.

The Slack house employs substantial areas of glazing. Some are protected by roof overhangs in the form of corner decks, others are located with respect to the canopy of trees that shades much of the lot in summer.

Cedar is used extensively inside and out to provide visual unity and warmth. And it *is* a warm house—angular, playful, inviting in its flow of space.

FIRST FLOOR

SECOND FLOOR

GARAGE

Architect, owner, contractor:
John Slack
5333 Raven Oaks Drive
Omaha, Nebraska
Photographer: Stephen Parezo

THE GRAY HOUSE

A house of immaculate, precise lines, this is an elegant expression that befits both entertaining and the down-to-earth functional necessity for a family of six. To fill the spatial needs for both privacy and interaction of family members, architect Paul Gray (of Warner and Gray architects) designed his own house as a "progression of spaces that move from large gathering areas to smaller more private ones, laced together with hallways."

To enhance privacy, the spaces are separated according to their function, reaching out in three directions from the entrance (upper right). The bedroom wing (right) which consumes the bulk of the 4,200 square feet, is to the north and is part of the family-centered areas, while the formal living room is completely set off to the south. This portion has the dominant geometric form of the house—the shed roof—angled to accommodate the yet-to-be-installed solar energy collector panels.

Because the house is located on a three-acre hillside site near the coast, the house is oriented to frame views in all directions—to the north, the mountains; to the south, the ocean; and surrounding the house, eucalyptus trees.

An integral part of the crispness of the design is the subtle separation of horizontal and vertical planes. Viewed from the exterior, the house appears to "float," being slightly raised on a concrete slab foundation and is recessed from the perimeter walls: this recess is visually emphasized by use of dark-colored stones around the base. This idea of articulation is expressed in the interiors through reveals at the junction of walls with floor and ceilings, painted a dark color, again for emphasis.

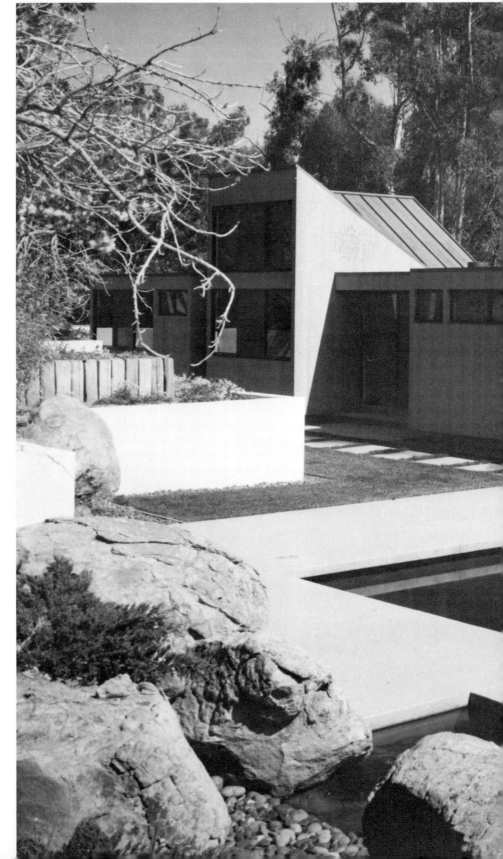

Architect: Paul Gray
  of Warner-Gray
  1225 Coast Village Road
  Santa Barbara, California
Owners: Mr. & Mrs. Paul Gray
Engineers:
  Theodore Anvick (structural/foundation)
  Leo Kummer (mechanical)
Landscape architects:
  Richard Harrington, Dick Gilbert, Paul Gray
Interior design:
  Paul Gray, Jack Warner, Gwen Warner
Contractor:
  A. O. Pieper (general)
Photographer: Charles White

One strong visual element in the design is a split fireplace (all photos left) which frames views of trees from the living room and maintains the proper scale for that section of the house, both inside and out. Of necessity, long hallways connect the multitude of rooms, but there is always a vista opened at the end, such as seen along the kitchen corridors (top and bottom). Clerestory windows abound, including in the family room (right).

THE CHAPELL HOUSE

The tall pines with their characteristically abstract profiles were both an amenity and a starting point for the design of this year-round vacation house that architect Donald Chapell built for his own use. To retain as many trees as possible—and to keep them as close to the house as he could—Chapell had to generate an intricate, multifaceted plan shape and develop it carefully for privacy and view.

To an unusual degree, the house is a single large space with alcoves—alcoves that can be closed off when necessary by sliding doors. On the lower level, the living room, lined on two sides by glass, is flanked on the other two sides by kitchen and master bedroom. Two more sleeping spaces are located upstairs and are linked by a bridge over the living room—a bridge that also serves to shade the sitting area below from direct sunlight admitted through the large expanses of glazing to the south. Even larger openings occur on the north and provide a balanced, glareless daylight as well as views to the site.

The house is framed in wood stud and finished in cedar siding laid up vertically. The scale and texture thus created are welcome on the broad planar surfaces but do not interfere with the shifting patterns of shadow cast by the pines overhead. The same siding is used at various places inside for continuity and texture.

For summer comfort, the house is open and cross-ventilation is carefully provided. Windows are recessed not only to protect them from the sun but so that they can be left open during rainy weather without disturbing the regular air flow through the house.

The Chapell house is fun. It is spatially lively yet easy to maintain. The principal furnishing elements are built-in without sacrifice to flexibility and the house can be used and enjoyed by owner and occupants in a variety of ways.

Architect and owner:
  Don Chapell
  24 East 73rd Street
  New York City
Contractor: John Caramagna
Photographer: Bernard Askienazy

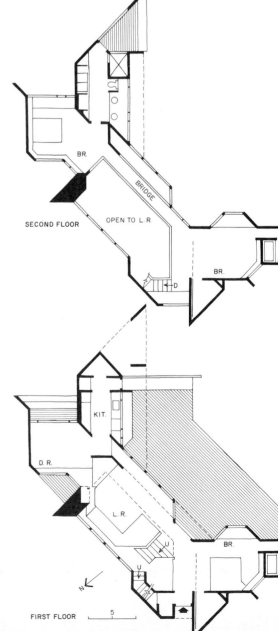

SECOND FLOOR

BR. BRIDGE OPEN TO L.R. BR.

KIT. D.R. L.R. BR.

FIRST FLOOR

Strings of red light bulbs (visible in the uppermost of the three small photos at left) are part of a larger lighting sequence that gives the interiors a warm rose glow during the evening. From outside on the deck, they make long, linear patterns that suggest, to the architect-owner, images of airport runways at night.

THE JAFFE HOUSE

The architect's own house and studio in Bridgehampton is a synthesis of the wood shingles, steeply-pitched roofs, dormers and chimneys that traditionally characterize regional houses in eastern Long Island. Though exaggerating these features in scale, the house stops safely short of burlesquing them, for nowhere are the functions of the house compromised by these exaggerations.

Stepping up under the roof at the intermediate levels are a complex series of spaces, Piranesian in conception and thrust, which house the regular range of domestic spaces. Under these, but not pressed down by them, is the architect's studio opposite, a double-height space filled with daylight from several sources. The uppermost level houses a master bedroom, bath and small study, from which the spatial composition is most fully revealed (photo left). The massive chimney includes a large skylight that brings daylight deep into the house.

Throughout the interiors, wood is used skillfully in ways that exploit its potential for warmth, color and pattern.

JAFFE HOUSE, Bridgehampton, Long Island, New York. Architect and contractor: *Norman Jaffe.*

SECOND LEVEL

FOURTH LEVEL

FIRST LEVEL

THIRD LEVEL

Interior walls of the Jaffe house are finished in cypress. Floors are Pennsylvania slate and pine. Major openings face east and west. The north and south elevations have limited exposures for high contrast and strong exterior shadows.

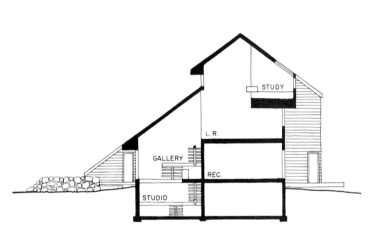

THE MAH HOUSE

Perhaps no project can cause an architect so much difficult consideration (or final joy) as his or her own house. It is a commission without the limitations, and consequent design directions, usually imposed by clients. While this fact alone can cause enough worry, the resulting freedom of choice produces a definitive result for the judgment of peers and potential clients. Architect Francis Mah — despite a well-proven track record as a designer — was not exempt from a long period of worried thought on the subject, thought that produced a formula for being his own client: The house would become a laboratory for testing some of his own long-held ideas about the general nature of what houses should be.

Located at the end of a long drive through pleasant woods, the Mah house seems serenely isolated from the densely-built Memphis suburbs that surround it. In fact — the neighbors are only a stone's throw away. The site is a long narrow ravine, subject to seasonal flooding, and Mah has turned a potential defect into an asset by simply diverting the periodic waters. Partially because of the closeness of the neighbors, the house looks inward, so that few of the areas have views directly to the outside. Instead, there is an elegant flow of space from most of the "traditional" spaces into a vast enclosed space that seems to be outdoors. Mah describes the concept as a house within a house.

There are other reasons for the concept than avoiding the neighbors' stares. In the spirit of testing ideas, the house first saves fuel through passive solar heating. The roof of the "outdoor" space is translucent plastic, which allows an enormous heat gain during sunny winter days. In a climate that can be harsh, tropical plants thrive year-round. The effect on "the inner house" is a fuel bill that can be a third that of a conventional house. Another idea that Mah is testing with his house is an alternative to traditional concepts of what is marketable. Surrounded by new houses that derive their forms from doubtful tradition, Mah has let his house derive its strong identity from its concept. And — as in all good laboratories — he is constantly fine tuning to effect a desired and eminently affordable result.

Because over half of the area is heated by passive solar means, architect Francis Mah has been able to build his own new house so that it is both dramatically spacious and economical in construction and maintenance. While there are over 7,000 square feet of area, approximately half of that area takes the form of the vast garden room seen in the photos here. The garden room acting as a solar collector is not only independent for its own heat, but it contributes strongly to the heating of the conventionally enclosed parts of the house as well. Another cost-saver is the use of economical materials frankly exposed to view, such as the corrugated metal roof. The wood-frame construction has a stucco finish on walls and the rough-sawn roof construction is left exposed within the interior, as the "outdoor" space acts as insulation. As seen in the photos, this space extends over the interior in the form of a loft. The concrete floors have been stained and are highly polished. Aided by a profusion of space and a truly grand scale seldom found in this "think-tight" era, the ordinary takes on a lavish quality. It is really

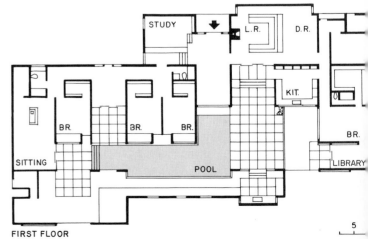

FIRST FLOOR

the flow of space that sets this house apart. The end effect is a timeless environment which Mah has heightened by the use of retrieved parts of older buildings, such as the entrance door and the mantle (see photos). While Mah may not have consciously set out to challenge the closed-in spaces and dubious style of many of the suburban houses around him, he has clearly shown that a truly fresh house can have both a indigenous and highly appropriate character. He has shown that such a house can be built of economical local materials, and that it can be what the others miss: undeniably elegant.

MAH HOUSE, Memphis, Tennessee. Owners: *Mr. and Mrs. Francis Mah.* Architects: *Walk Jones & Francis Mah, Inc.* Engineers: *Reeves Engineering (structural/foundations/soils); Herschel L. Powell & Associates (mechanical/electrical).* General contracting by the architects.

4

Vacation houses, planned for a relaxed kind of living, often generate a special kind of design excitement

Vacation houses are often very special—and there is often much to learn from them. They are usually small—yet they seem to have plenty of room. They are typically relaxed and informal and easier to care for than "the main house"—and everyone enjoys that. (Any lesson for "everyday living" there?) They are usually built on very modest budgets—and it is easy to wonder why so many vacation houses are really much nicer than the more expensive, more finished houses the families come from. It is true that in most residential design competitions—the American Institute of Architects Honor Award programs and the Homes for Better Living competition sponsored by McGraw-Hill's *Housing* magazine—a very high proportion of the winners are vacation houses. And why is that? What can we learn from that? Perhaps that design for fun is more important than some image of formality that seems to be required back in town. Perhaps that the disciplines normally imposed by vacation-house clients—tight budget, low maintenance, simple materials —are useful design constraints for architects in designing houses.

The vacation house on the next pages was not just designed by architect Robert Kindorf for his own family—it was actually built by his family. It is a tiny thing, without electricity and with very minimal plumbing, heated by a wood-burning stove, with minimal finishes and detailing. But nonetheless it is a very special house—carefully designed around a simple and clearly logical structure, and indeed quite beautiful.

The Bystrom house (page 90) also built by the family, is even smaller, and incorporates some extraordinary ideas. Item: the roof is transparent plastic, which of course lets in an extraordinary amount and quality of light even on the rainy days which abound at the Washington State shore (at which time the roof also collects water). This is a beautiful, award-winning house—not for everyone, but worth study by everyone for its ideas and its spirit.

The Williams house (page 92) explores an often-dreamed-of option for a vacation house—remodeling a barn (in fact, two of them linked together). But architect Williams took an approach that deserves careful attention by other barn-fanciers: he restored the barns, leaving their materials and finishes and structure intact; then added the "new" that was needed—a connecting link, new circulation space, new floors and furniture—in a crisply contemporary way. He consciously avoided "a contrived and sentimental comingling" of old and new; instead left the old strictly alone and added in a perfectly clear way the new that was needed. And that is a concept that deserves attention from others.

Architect Dmitri Vedensky's house at Sea Ranch (page 96) explores another concept of vacation living—exceedingly modest in form and materials on the exterior, inside it is handled as one big room—with only the bathroom enclosed. It is not a form of living that would be comfortable for everyone, but it clearly pleases the Vedenskys—which is what a good architect-designed house is all about.

Their own house on Fire Island (Long Island, New York) by Judith and Richard Newman is another deceptively simple-looking "box"—but it is animated by a lively and informal plan with rooms on no less than seven levels and an extraordinary screened indoor-outdoor space that provides a pleasant blurring between the enclosed spaces and the outdoors.

Architect Ulrich Franzen's house near the beach on Long Island explores a very different approach to summer living—it is a crisp white house set on piles above possible high water, and with a selection of outdoor decks—a "choice intended to lure people outside no matter what the sun or wind conditions."

A house designed by architect Ray Crites is miles away from these beach houses in both physical distance (it is in Iowa) and philosophy. Crites chose a steep portion of his wooded site and created a house that blends into the hillside with almost no excavation. The house is small (1,654 square feet) and narrow (only 12 feet)—but walls of glass and cantilevered decks and greenhouses open the house spacially—and to a very pleasant kind of outdoor living.

The final project in this chapter is really very special: a series of pavilions on the Oregon beach used not just by the owner-architect, but with separate spaces for employee or client families and a lodge for group meetings. It is a wonderful kind of retreat—says architect Stephen Johnston: "It is another world—a world I wish we could share with all." Which is a pretty good way to feel about your vacation place—whether it is on an Oregon beach or in an Iowa meadow....

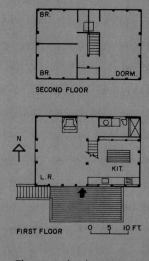

SECOND FLOOR

FIRST FLOOR

The upper level contains bedrooms with a dormitory character. The middle level, reached from the bedrooms by a stairladder, includes living, dining, kitchen and bath. The lowest level (not shown in plan) is an equipment storage area with an earthen floor.

THE KINDORF HOUSE

Without power tools, without heavy equipment, without, in fact, outside help of any important kind, the Kindorf family, five-strong, built this appealing, three-level cabin on a two-acre site in Plumas County, California. The site is choked with pine and dips down to a large creek where swimming and trout fishing are seasonal preoccupations. The cabin was built over a period of three summers with cabinetwork and furniture construction occupying the long winter months in between.

The cabin has no electricity. Light is provided by kerosene lamps and heat by a Franklin stove. A 500-gallon, gravity-fed water tank supplies domestic needs and sewage wastes are chemically treated and stored. The absence of modern conveniences is in no way deprivative, for the family agrees that the simplified life style that results is fun and greatly heightens the sense of place.

Clad in cedar board and batten over plywood sheathing and 4- by 4-inch wood studs, the cabin has a simplicity and structural logic plainly visible in the photos. Its living and sleeping arrangements have a pleasant informality and its detailing and finishes are minimal.

Because of its inherent modesty and the very special circumstances surrounding its construction, the Kindorf cabin was built for the astonishingly low figure of $5 per square foot.

Architect and owner: Robert Kindorf
245 Draeger Drive
Moraga, California
Location: Plumas County, California
Contractors: The Kindorf family
Photographer: Philip Molten

To ease the erection process, Kindorf framed out the floors in doubled 2x6s, bolted in place, and the roof in 2x8s, also paired. Floor planking is white fir, roof is galvanized sheet.

THE BYSTROM HOUSE

Arne Bystrom photos

This vacation house for a family of four is a tiny little cube—about 17 feet square and two stories high. But it is a tiny place packed with innovative ideas, with pleasant and well-zoned living spaces, with energy-conserving features—and with personality.

The house was built by the Bystrom family themselves on a stunning site (photo below)—a remote three-acre plot on Washington State's Olympic Peninsula. Architect Bystrom wisely made no attempt to compete with the site—the over-scale shakes on the exterior blend completely into the wooded hillside.

Inside, the main living spaces—the living room, the dining room, and the kitchen—all open to each other, all open through sliding glass doors to small decks and the broad spaces beyond, and are all brightened and given larger scale by glimpses of the sky through the most unusual roof. The roof eave is set diagonally across the enclosed space, and from the eave the rafters reach out to the walls in an interesting set of V-patterns (photo upper right). The roof itself is acrylic, letting light (and solar energy) into all the rooms. The two sleeping lofts on the second level are reached by ladders.

Water is collected from the roof, stored in a large wooded barrel on a second-level outdoor platform (see upper-level plan) and piped to the kitchen. The "bath" is an outhouse. Whenever enough heat has not been generated through the passive solar collector—i.e., the roof—a wood-burning stove quickly warms both levels.

BYSTROM HOUSE, Olympic Peninsula, Washington. Architect, owner, builder, and photographer: *Arne Bystrom, AIA.*

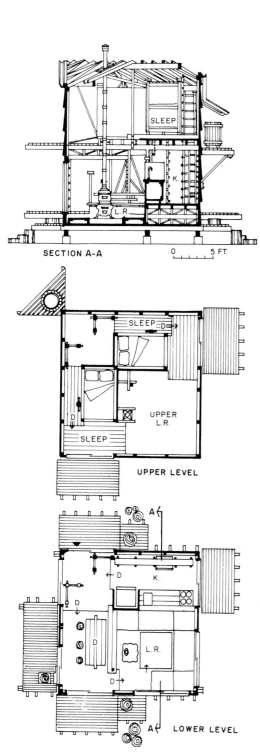

SECTION A-A

0   5 FT.

UPPER LEVEL

LOWER LEVEL

The plans show a compact but eminently usable and comfortable plan. On the lower level, small changes in floor level help define the main living, dining, and kitchen areas. Light pours into this level not just through sliding glass, but from the acrylic roof far above. Both the living room and the "stair tower" at the opposite corner open to the roof; the dining space and the kitchen have a lower scale under the sleeping lofts.

This house won a First Honor Award in *Housing's* Homes for Better Living competition.

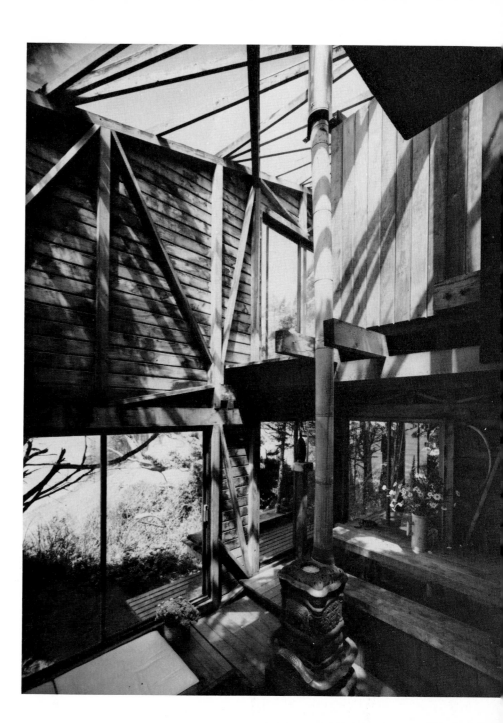

THE WILLIAMS HOUSE

A ramshackle potato barn on eastern Long Island is something short of an important architectural legacy. But Tod Williams saw in this humble artifact more than the picturesque remnant of a lost rural landscape: he saw both the form and the structure of the barn as "possessing an inherent integrity worth preserving and defining as an element" within a larger composition.

The larger composition was to be an assemblage of readily discernible parts that would include a second barn (moved to the site from a nearby farm), a simple corridor between the two barns, and various service modules and partitions to make the spaces function as a house. Williams believes that the success of the project hinged on his ability to express and articulate the divisibility of these components. And looking at the house, one has the uncanny sensation that objects were individually dropped into place and could be effortlessly separated again. This system is reinforced diagrammatically—everything old is unadorned wood, and everything new is painted white.

The juxtaposition of the crisp white additions and the weathered wood of the barns creates a visual tension which contrasts both the separateness and the relationship of the parts—the barns become more barn-like against the icy white plastic laminate of the bathrooms and kitchen, and the rigid sym-

After assembling the two-barn house (photo above) for himself, Williams repeated the process across the field with a three-barn house (see site plan) that he intended to sell. At first glance, the two houses appear to be twins and their resemblance is intriguing enough to make closer inspection irresistible. But rather than being diminished by comparison, the similarities serve to give each house a more articulate sense of autonomy.

Rather than insulate the roof from the underside, Williams opted to cover the old roof with stiff foam and then rebuild a duplicate roof on top. The advantage of this more expensive method was that the character of the old barn was unaltered. Insulating the walls was handled in the same way where the shingles were decayed; where the shingles were still good, the insulation was put inside and covered with oak planks.

metry of the modules and partitions becomes even more sculptural when played against the pockmarked wood beams. The unaltered simplicity of the barn form and the distinct clarity of the new construction are, for Williams, legitimate forms of preservation and intervention; especially appropriate because the delineation between old and new must be underscored if the integrity of the barn and the purity of the new construction are to be left intact.

The flat-roofed corridor that connects the two barns serves to articulate each as separate while joining them as one. This heavily glazed, almost transparent link is bisected by a concrete cylinder that serves pragmatically as a flue for the underground furnace, and symbolically as a column to signal the primary entrance.

The original barn doors have been left on their tracks and are still operable: the void they create when open is taken up by a door and double-hung windows with a variety of mullions intended to relate to the various scales of the buildings. During the winter, the barn doors can be closed for added insulation.

This barn/house structure begins with the premise that new is new and old is old, and the line that separates the two is to be rigorously respected. With the exception of skylights and replacement windows, the old barns have been left alone. For Williams, the other, untenable option was to make the composition a contrived and ''sentimental'' commingling of intrinsically disparate elements that would be compromised if their distinctiveness were blurred. And for this architect, the resultant ambiguity would be a loss of significance.

Tod Williams is not the first architect to recognize the domestic potential of a barn. But what distinguishes this project is that the qualities that make a barn appealing have not only survived, but been enhanced by renovation.

WILLIAMS RESIDENCE, Sagaponack, New York. Architects: *Tod Williams & Associates—principal-in-charge: Tod Williams; assistant, Billie Tsien.* Contractor: *ELP Construction.*

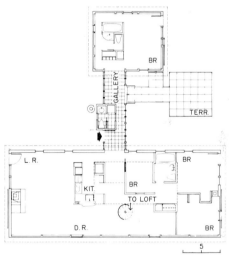

THE VEDENSKY HOUSE

This vacation house at the Sea Ranch in California is built on a heavily wooded site on a hill above Sea Ranch's well-publicized meadows. Except for one small swath cut through to allow a view of the distant ocean, the site feels private, and the windows open onto views of the adjacent trees.

Consequently the exterior of the house (photo right) has been kept as simple as possible ("You can barely see it from most directions," the architect points out), and the form, too, is nothing more than one large box with a sloping roof, with two bedroom lean-to's.

Inside, though, there are surprises. For one thing there are two large skylights in the roof above the shower room and the kitchen area (seen in the bottom photos on the opposite page). These admit not just light, but direct light into the house—moving and changing with the hour and the seasons, and contrasting with the dappled sunbeams that filter through the trees and enter through the windows.

The architect has also made a considerable point of the variety of activities and moods that can be accommodated in the one big room of his house. The toilet, for instance, is in the only space that is completely enclosed, and the guest bedroom (seen in the background of the photo below right) is, when unoccupied, open to the living area by a vertically-sliding *shoji,* and separated from the seats around the fireplace only by a *tatami* platform for sitting (without the aid of chairs) or sleeping (without beds) or for meditating.

Above the *tatami* platform are two sleeping lofts reached by a vertical ladder. They are open to the large room below, as is the bathing area (behind the wall in the bottom left photo opposite). The act of bathing is enlivened by a large wooden Japanese bathtub, by a shower and by a view from the shower room to the outside, through sliding glass doors that open onto a deck.

With all these blandishments the house invites the joyful liberations of vacation-house living. It even has a Moon Gate (photo right). Why? "Just because I like Moon Gates," the architect says.

Architect and owner: Dmitri Vedensky
2262 Mason Street
San Francisco, California
Location: Sea Ranch, California
Contractor: Harold Halvorsen
Photographer: Gerald K. Lee

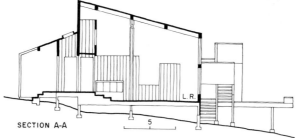

SECTION A-A

The section above shows the shape of the one large room, and of one of the bedroom lean-to's. The main entrance is on the left; decks, platforms and Moon Gate are shown on the right.

96

THE NEWMAN HOUSE

Husband and wife architects Richard and Judith Newman designed this remarkable summer house for themselves and their children on a corner lot in Saltaire, Fire Island, New York. The scrub pine that grows so thickly on the site masks the elevations and provides a dense curtain of privacy—especially on the lower levels of the house where tufted greenery feels almost like an interior finish.

The square, 32- by 32-foot plan is complicated by seven distinct interior levels. The desirable functional separations that result (see plan) provide a lively volumetric flow that invites rather than inhibits movement throughout the house. As a reflection of the Newman's informal summer lifestyle, the kitchen/dining space occupies a prime location in the spatial hierarchy as it overlooks major living spaces and opens across a narrow deck to long views of island and water. Another unusual feature of the house is a double-height, screened portico with a deliberately ambiguous indoor/outdoor character that encloses several trees and provides overflow play space.

Most furniture in the house is built in—a design imperative for this island site. Finishes have been omitted where they are not necessary. The house has no soffits or ceilings. Where finishes are required, they have been selected for their durability. The detailing has an agreeable simplicity throughout. Yet the results are anything but spartan. The Newman house is colorful, comfortable, inventive, carefully sited (the builder tied back trees to apply exterior siding) and most important of all—fun. Like the trees it has captured, the Newman house has made happy captives of its owners who spend every moment they can in their ingratiating new surroundings.

NEWMAN HOUSE, Fire Island, New York, Architects and owners: *Richard and Judith Newman.* Structural engineer: *J. Ames.* Contractor: *Joseph Chasas;* Photographer: *William Maris.*

UPPER LEVELS

LOWER LEVELS

In keeping with the rough, unfinished character of the house, the Newmans have used open shelving for a wide variety of storage requirements. With generous openings on all elevations, the house makes the most of summer breezes from any quarter—an obvious virtue on this Fire Island site.

Quarry tile, used on counters, is one of the few indulgences.

The double-height, screened portico with its hostage trees opens to the upper living room through a sliding window assembly for ventilation as well as for supervision of children's play.

Trees receive almost as much daylight now as they did before.

THE FRANZEN HOUSE

New code restrictions stipulated that the first floor of this vacation house, which is adjacent to wetlands and in an area subject to periodic hurricane flooding, be lifted 15 feet over mean high water—in this case some ten feet over existing grade. The architect, building for himself, sought to "float the house over a sea of bayberry bushes," supporting the structure on an 11- by 13-foot grid of pressure-treated piles. 3-inch by 12-inch girders form the primary deck structure. This frame is braced by steel tubes and by X-bracing below. Roof loads are carried down to this deck structure by stud walls and hollow steel columns. The complete 40- by 60-foot volume cantilevers two and a half feet beyond the pilings.

While the house is winterized, it is intended chiefly as a summer and weekend retreat. Four different decks for viewing or sunbathing have been provided: one at the entry, a second on the northwest corner, a third off the living/dining area and a fourth on the roof. The choice is intended to lure people outside no matter what the sun or wind conditions.

The enclosed space adds up to only about 1650 square feet. The rooms are gently defined and most open generously to the various views without sacrifice to privacy where needed. In shaping these spaces, Franzen responded to the sweeping horizontality of the site, its foreground vistas of low, dense greenery, and the all but unlimited horizon of water beyond. The principal finishes are vertical tongue-and-groove cedar boards for exterior siding, half-inch gypsum board for most interior partitioning, carpeting for floors, cedar paneling for ceilings, redwood decking outdoors and a 5-ply bituminous built-up roof. All windows are double glazed.

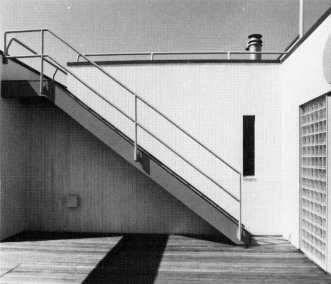

Architect and owner: Ulrich Franzen
   555 Madison Avenue
   New York City
Project architect: David Acheson
Engineers: Geiger-Berger Associates (structural)
   A.F. Turk & Son (custom metalwork)
Contractor: Laszlo Girhiny
Photographer: David Franzen©ESTO photos

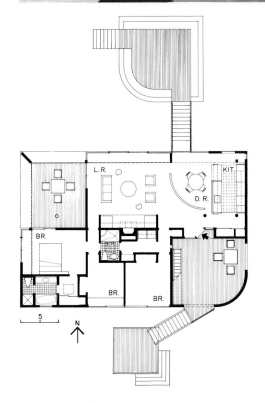

Julius Shulman photos

THE CRITES HOUSE

This house is notched into a steep (35- to 40-degree) hillside—and thus all rooms on both levels have an extraordinary tree-house feeling. To minimize grading on the hillside, and minimize damage to trees (only one tree was removed) the house is only 12 feet wide. But all of the living spaces are made more spacious and brightened by the outdoor spaces off each room. On the upper level, both the bedroom and the study have big decks open through sliding glass doors (the study deck is seen in the photo above). The rooms on the lower level are made special by the most distinctive feature of the house (see both interior photos, at right)—a wall of glass with two greenhouse areas that extend out six feet and open up the relatively narrow rooms. These greenhouse spaces, which are used as dining-sitting space, have a passive solar function as well. In the winter they are closed off by translucent, double-walled acrylic panels that cut heat loss at night.

Outside the main living area, a triangular deck reaches out beyond the "greenhouse" for a large summer living area open to the south and the best view.

CRITES HOUSE, Huxley, Iowa. Architect: *Ray Crites.* Contractor: *Buck Construction.*

The Crites house is designed as a series of strong planes of wood in natural finishes, with the decks extended out as trays. It is a contemporary form, set off by the square stair tower (photo right) joining the two levels.

The plan shows a simple and logical grouping of spaces within the narrow shape of the house. All major rooms are opened up with sliding glass to wide decks—and the main living/dining space is given drama (and solar heat) by finely detailed greenhouse extensions. The area of the house is only 1654 square feet.

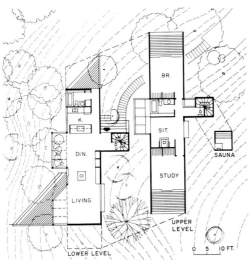

UPPER LEVEL

LOWER LEVEL

0 5 10 FT.

BR.

SIT.

SAUNA

STUDY

K.

DIN.

LIVING

THE TRAVERS/JOHNSTON HOUSE

On the central Oregon coast at Salishan a beach house complex, designed by and for the architectural office of Travers/Johnston as a retreat, has been successfully created as "another world . . . a world I wish we could share with all," says Stephen Johnston. As a tribute to the delightful character of the retreat, it has been in almost constant use by the architects and employees and their families, clients and friends.

Located on the end lot of a spit of land separating Siletz Bay from the Pacific Ocean,

the site has a commanding and uninterrupted 270 degree view of water. After the idea of a retreat was decided upon, the office staff was asked for suggestions with the final design concept being derived from many "bull sessions." The two major requirements were that it must be a retreat which would allow places for solitude as well as group gatherings, and that it accommodate several families at the same time. This need for a variety of spaces spurred the idea of an octagonal lodge and three hexagonal bedroom units (or modules), grouped in

The lodge (left), as the center for most group activities, has the only kitchen, dining and lounge areas. Changes in floor level, expressed in carpet-covered concrete steps, form seating around the fire-pit and contribute to the informality of the room. The bedroom modules are identical. Two modules have views of dunes and one has an ocean view.

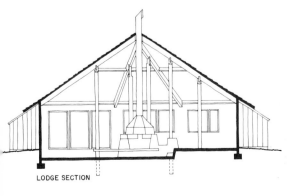

LODGE SECTION

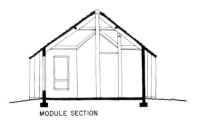

MODULE SECTION

a circle to create a central courtyard onto which all doors open. The focal point of the courtyard is a sunken area where guests can sit around an open fire-pit. Two decks on the ocean side provide space for sunning. A basement under one module ("Bay" on plan) serves as boat shed, laundry and storage area.

At the angles of each unit are fins extending outward. This element of the design is a strong exterior feature, visually unifying the buildings and serving as a partial windscreen against the strong and almost constant winds.

The exterior is of resawn cedar with a roof of cedar shingles. To capture the magnificent views of land and water and to allow as much light as possible to enter on the foggy and stormy days that are so much a part of the Northwest coast's weather, glass doors and many large windows are used. Glass partitions between units also serve as additional windscreens and open up views to the courtyard. The largest of the modules, the lodge, provides such necessary community facilities as kitchen, eating and lounging areas. Smooth cedar

is used on interior walls, resawn hemlock on the ceiling. The communal character of the project is emphasized by the fact that the whole complex was not only designed but built by the architects and their staff.

BEACH HOUSE-RETREAT, Salishan, Glenedon Beach, Oregon. Architects: *Travers/Johnston.* Engineers: *MacKenzie Engineering Inc.* (structural), *Hugh L. Langton & Associates* (electrical), *McGinnis Engineering Inc.* (mechanical). Interiors: *Travers/Johnston.* Landscape architect: *William Teufel.* Contractor: *Trajon Corporation.*

An exhilarating site for a retreat,
the Salishan Spit is sand dunes
stabilized by pines, grasses and
logs swept onto the beaches.
Comprising 2000 sq ft, the retreat does not intrude on the
area. The only landscaping
needed was to reestablish native grasses and pines surrounding the complex.

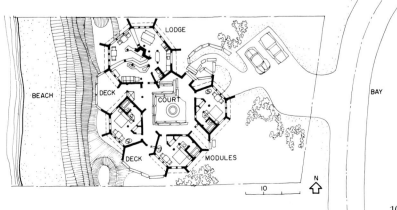

5

Houses for hot climates explore ways to live comfortably when it is very hot—and that can occur almost anywhere

With the great migration to the Sun Belt, and especially to the Southwest, more and more families will find themselves concerned with the design of houses in climates where—most of the time, as the old song goes—it's too darn hot.

And at a time where overpowering the weather conditions with massive air conditioning systems is increasingly expensive as power rates rise, it perhaps behooves even those of us who live in more moderate climates (where, for much of the summer, it is still uncomfortably hot) to consider the designs of talented architects who have solved these problems in terms of their own family living.

There are just three houses in this chapter. They are very different—the two desert houses take very different approaches to the climate, and the house on St. Thomas, Virgin Islands, of course grows from altogether different roots. Nonetheless, in the cause of coolness, they have some things in common: all are essentially one-room deep, inviting the cooling breezes through the house whenever they are available. In all of them, the big glass areas designed to open to that breeze are sheltered from the sun. All of them have outdoor spaces to take advantage of the views—but they are artfully shaded from the sun. They are an interesting, if special, study—full of ideas, again, that might serve all of us well even though we do not live in the desert or on a sub-tropical island.

And finally, there are signs of appropriate fun. The painted plywood flowers at architect Fred Osmon's house are indeed a "mock-defiant gesture" to the surrounding desert, and are bound to make everyone approaching it feel good. Which is another thing that good custom houses are all about....

The Osmon House in Carefree, Arizona is described on the following pages.

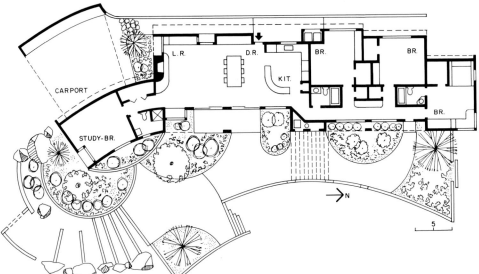

THE OSMON HOUSE

Osmon's own house is located in the badlands of southwest Arizona. The design is an investigation of the relationship between house and desert as well as a series of comments, some of them whimsical, others mildly reproachful, on the nature of that relationship. The painted plywood flowers and rocks, for instance, are a delicious mock-defiant gesture but add unexpected and welcome color on the approach to the house. A more laconic comment is the placement and treatment of the condenser unit (photos bottom right). Painted bright blue and made a feature on the terrace, the condenser is a surrender-with-style to desert reality—and perhaps a reproof to those who think that living comfortably with daytime temperatures of 120 degrees is simply a matter of manipulating a few simple, native devices. It is not, as Osmon will tell you, quite as easy as that.

The house is built in masonry and redwood, one of the few woods that stands up well in this climate. Though not large, the interiors feel ample, even spacious. The sloped ceiling adds height at one side and the curves at soffit, at the fireplace, and at the kitchen counters add considerable visual interest. The long curve is reflected on the east elevation of the house where the gentle arc gives just a suggestion of enclosure without interrupting the 180-degree view from the terrace. The retaining wall undulates playfully to echo the distant mountains and supports a simple overhead trellis also of redwood.

With a freestanding arch to mark and dignify its approach but with no front door to signal arrival, the Osmon house states its designer's priorities in often unexpected fashion. But behind this playfulness, it is a house extremely well suited to its beautiful but somewhat inhospitable environment and to the functional requirements placed on it by its architect/owner.

Architect: Fred Linn Osmon
Box 1454
Carefree, Arizona
Engineer: Yury Sheydayi (structural)
Photographer: Joshua Freiwald

The living/dining space (photos left) serves as a buffer between the three bedrooms to the north and the guest quarters and carport to the south. All spaces are linked by a long, single-loaded corridor (photo above.)

THE BRUDER HOUSE

This modest house, carefully sited in a relatively empty stretch of desert north of Phoenix, was designed by its owner and constructed with the help of friends in just over a month, using the simplest kinds of materials and details. A good deal of forethought and invention went into its planning, however. The result is an unusually expressive small house and studio that are fine-tuned to the climate and constructed for under $13,000—or roughly eleven dollars per square foot – some five years ago.

The house is conventionally framed in wood stud with 2 x 10 floor joists supporting a fiberboard subfloor. The roof structure is composed of 3 x 8 fir beams on four-foot centers. Insulation is applied throughout: four-inch batts in the stud walls and a two-inch thickness of rigid urethane under the red roll roofing. The exterior, though, is unexpectedly clad in galvanized metal sheet. Because it is corrugated and matte finished, it does not throw off eye-searing reflections under the bright sun. Instead, it produces softly-glowing reflections of the surrounding desert—reflections that change perceptibly as the days and seasons pass.

To the right in the plan (above) is a small drafting studio with two work spaces. Opposite the studio, across the entry breezeway, is the main living space, which also doubles for dining and sleeping. It backs against a kitchen, bath and dressing area. Nearly every space is detailed for multiple use.

Unifying the two halves of the structure is a generously-scaled, trellised deck that faces a deep arroyo and undisturbed natural desert beyond. Here is the outdoor center of activity, a space for a wide variety of uses day or night. This north exposure is completely glazed while the openings on the other three elevations are sharply controlled against the sun.

Space conditioning is achieved by an evaporative cooling unit with exposed ducts and a fireplace augmented by portable heaters for winter evenings.

Architect and owners:
  Mr. & Mrs. William P. Bruder
  Black Canyon Stage
  New River, Arizona
Photographer: Neil Koppes

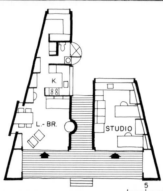

The shallow pitch of the roof is echoed in the tapered plan shapes which open to the north. The large glazed opening is shielded from the sun by an overhead trellis that casts elaborate shadow patterns across the deck and side walls.

Tom Yee photos

THE BATES HOUSE

"The nicest 3 million dollar,* 3-room house I've ever lived in" is the way architect Harry Bates jokingly describes the house he designed for himself on the island of St. Thomas in the U.S. Virgin Islands. Sited on a mountainside at an elevation of about 1000 feet, the house is oriented toward the west, toward the ocean and distant views of Puerto Rico on the horizon. Whether it is a "tropical house" in the generally understood sense of that term is a moot question. It was Bates' intention to reinterpret the oldest and most enduring West Indian houses which were traditionally built of wood. But rather than the shutters and blinds of these earlier houses, he protected the large expanses of glass with deep overhangs, wood lattices and screens. The house, therefore, has an inner, glazed lining that can be thrown open to catch the breezes whenever comfort dictates. In the fashion of houses throughout the

*Not quite, of course, but Bates describes building costs in the islands as "shocking" —approximately twice those in many similar U.S. areas.

DECK

UP

DECK

UP

N

5

The entry (photo above) is across a short bridge and into the gazebo. Potted plants, inside and out, soften the demarcation between house and site. Dining space, shown left, occurs in the long gallery that forms the eastern perimeter of the house.

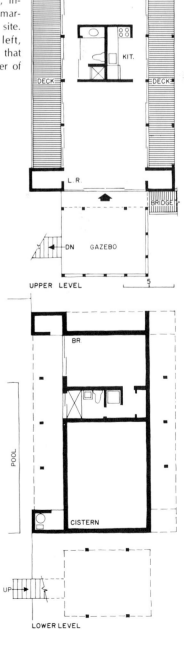

UPPER LEVEL

LOWER LEVEL

islands, rainwater is collected on the roof and conveyed by leaders to a cistern under the house where it is filtered for purity and stored for later use.

The simple rectangular massing was a compromise with the difficulty of the terrain and the cost of building in this somewhat remote region. The house rests on foundations of reinforced block surfaced with stucco. The pool deck, entry and gazebo are constructed using cypress decking. Exterior siding and interior partitions, ceilings and soffits are finished in fir plywood. The roof structure is 2-by 6-in. T&G fir decking. Surfaces subjected to the weather are treated for protection against termites and stained off-white.

The interiors are treated pleasantly in simple spatial volumes. The house is not large—1100 square feet enclosed—but space expanding

devices, like a mirrored living room wall, are used to advantage. Living, dining, kitchen, master bedroom and bath occupy the upper level. Cistern, guest bedroom and bath share the lower level. The levels are connected by an outside stair from the gazebo down to the pool deck on the western side of the house. Inside and out, the detailing is simple but elegant.

From all appearances, it is an exceptionally comfortable low-maintenance house that employs a limited vocabulary of forms and materials to create a gracious but unpretentious setting for life in the sub-tropics.

BATES HOUSE, St. Thomas, U.S. Virgin Islands. Architect and owner: *Harry Bates*. Engineer: *F. R. McCloskey* (structural). Consultant: *Martin Kopp* (structural). Contractors: *Crouse-Hampton, Inc.*

On the north side of the house, at right angles to the direction of the slope, Bates has developed a small terrace protected from the sun. The master bedroom (photo right) with a strip window over the headboard, overlooks the terrace and opens, at the side, into a covered gallery.

6

Apartments designed by architects for their own use offer some special lessons in the use of space...

...lessons in making the most of a space that has many constraints. For one thing, since apartments are being fitted into existing buildings, the essential space is fixed—though sometimes non-load-bearing partitions can be moved. Typically, compared to a house, the square footage is small. Often, in response to high-rise structural systems, the space is interrupted by columns. Usually, apartments have only one or two window walls—so natural light is limited; and many apartments are long and narrow, creating very special lighting problems.

And yet, within these limitations, architects are often able to create space that has all of the excitement and drama of a spectacular custom house. In the six apartments shown in this chapter—designed by architects for their own use—we see a variety of techniques for creating a *sense* of space where real spaciousness does not exist: In his apartment (photo right and following pages), architect Ulrich Franzen was able to replace a number of non-load-bearing walls with low partitions that opened up the space and let light flow deep into the apartment. Franzen had the special advantage of a penthouse location. Architect Randolph Croxton created thoroughly contemporary spaces within the confines of a turn-of-the-century townhouse —retaining a few handsome older details (like the ceiling moldings) and mixing them skillfully with contemporary detailing, art, and furniture (see pages 132-133). Architect Alan Buchsbaum transformed loft space in a former factory building into his living unit (pages 124-127). Here, space was generous—25 by 90 feet—and the problem was to define special spaces and living areas with furniture, with changes in level, with space dividers, and with very special attention to lighting. In sharp contrast to the spacious Buchsbaum loft, architect Michael Rubin fitted out a tiny apartment as carefully as the interior of a yacht. Everything is built in—and the "bedroom" is even tucked in as a second level above Rubin's working space (pages 128-129). Architect Paul Rudolph is known for using his personal living space as a "laboratory of ideas." He has since moved on from the apartment shown on pages 130-131, but the unit shown here makes astonishing use of changes in level, of special lighting, and of reflective and curved surfaces. Perhaps the most elegant example is the apartment of New York designers Massimo and Lella Vignelli. They transformed a large duplex in a 1909 apartment building into a series of highly varied but all very elegant spaces—furnished with furniture and art of their own design.

The lessons to be learned from apartments are lessons in making something very special out of sometimes-very-difficult constraints....

*Living room
of the Franzen apartment,
described on the next pages.*

THE FRANZEN APARTMENT

Norman McGrath photos

Once a dark "rabbit warren" of rooms that were a haunt of colorful Mayor Jimmy Walker, architect Ulrich Franzen's penthouse apartment is today spacious and filled with natural light. According to Franzen, the obvious advantage of a penthouse is that it can be designed almost independently from the rest of the building, like a "house in the sky." Accordingly, many of the original walls were replaced by low partitions. Overhead glazing, which admits the brightest south light, was introduced in the darkest room. Small exterior doors onto the north terrace were greatly widened to provide an eye-level view of a nearby church's dome, which becomes a strong decorative element. The raised library area is used for ordinary living-room functions, and overlooks what Franzen refers to as the "parlor" (foreground, photo overleaf) used for entertaining. But as opposed to parlors of the past, the room is finished *less* conventionally than the rest of the apartment and most clearly satisfies friends' and clients' expectations of a noted designer's lifestyle. Chromed metal covers the one visible column.

FRANZEN APARTMENT, New York, New York. Architect: *Ulrich Franzen.* Engineers: *Andrew Eliot* (structural); *Aaron Zichman* (mechanical). General contractor: *Van Hyning Construction Company.*

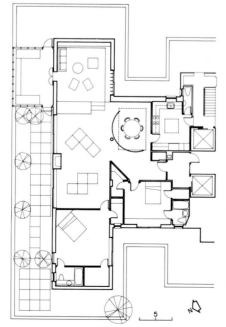

The remaining element of the original apartment, a former north-facing greenhouse next to the library, is now Franzen's office for work at home. All of the rest of the rooftop structure was almost totally rebuilt within the existing structure. The surrounding higher buildings form an enormous room in which the "house on top of a building" gains a sense of containment that is unusual for a penthouse.

THE BUCHSBAUM LOFT

Norman McGrath photos

At the time of purchase, this five-story loft building—a former cord factory—in Lower Manhattan showed many of the signs of neglect that make this kind of building economically attractive and certain design idiocyncracies that might be turned into architectural virtues. The floors were in poor condition and needed patching. The stamped tin ceiling, nailed right to the wood joists, was in sad disrepair. Transverse partitions, some of them awkwardly positioned with respect to the structural grid of heavy timber, chopped up the space wastefully. In addition, all the mechanical and plumbing services were at one end of the 25- by 90-foot floors.

Buchsbaum removed the partitions and made repairs to finishes where necessary. He opened the space to its full length. In plan, he zoned out the principal functions, being guided by obvious requirements for light and privacy. The kitchen, needing large amounts of neither, was placed near the center of one of the long walls. But to bring the services to it from the rear wall, the bedroom and dining areas had to be raised up to create a false floor. Across from the kitchen, Buchsbaum set up a work area with drafting tables, tack space and supply cabinets. The plan is completed by living space and bedroom at opposite ends.

In general feeling, the loft is casual and unselfconscious, although sculptural accents —as at the long kitchen counter—betray an abiding concern for form. Most of the furnishings are simple, informal, and selected for their potential for easy rearrangement. Buchsbaum has gotten considerable design mileage from subtle contrasts in textures and from a lighting plan that is well thought out and inventive in its selection of fixtures.

The bedroom however, presents a somewhat different vocabulary of form and finish—a vocabulary of more studied elegance and more dramatic contrasts (see preceding page). The raised floor is finished in a smooth, high glaze, off-white tile that turns up at the built-in bed to form an enclosure for the mattress. The closet has mirror-glass doors and the whole space is defined in the long axis by a gently undulating glass block partition that slaloms leisurely around a pair of heavy wood columns. The lighting is subdued in the bedroom although the glass block partition is actually lighted from both sides. A row of airport fixtures, floor mounted with rigid conduit and fitted with blue bulbs, lends the space an unexpected trace of mystery.

The building has three owners (Buchsbaum is one) and each occupies a floor. To put the project on a sounder economic footing, the remaining space has been turned into rental property.

LOFT FOR ALAN BUCHSBAUM, New York City. Architects: *Alan Buchsbaum and Stephen Tilly.* Lighting design: *Paul Marantz.*

The raised platform—required for plumbing—provides carpeted seating for the dining table which is set in a circular cutout. Over the dining area (photo at right) is a tapestry/sculpture executed in felt and designed by Robert Morris. The bath, with its open shower, is shown reflected (photo below). It is finished, like the bedroom, in reflective materials.

THE RUBIN APARTMENT

The original renovation of this 1850s brownstone established a one-bedroom apartment, but as the bedroom was only seven by eight feet—with an 11-foot ceiling, Rubin subdivided the space horizontally creating a sleeping loft above and a work space under. In the main space, he removed the massive marble mantle, rebuilt the fireplace wall and removed that portion of the bedroom wall that intersected the window wall.

In the space created by this series of adjustments, Rubin designed and installed a handsome seating area and table unit. The latter, which includes low cabinets, was covered in white plastic laminate. Other cabinets along the fireplace wall house hi-fi equipment and concealed lighting. To add space to his apartment, Rubin also decked the roof of the projecting sun porch below and thereby developed a narrow but welcome terrace.

The result is a tidy, contemporary and surprisingly comfortable living space fashioned with wit out of what was little more than remnants from the past.

PRIVATE APARTMENT, New York City. Architect: *Michael Rubin.* Cabinetry: *Gene Black (Materials Design Workshop).*

Norman McGrath photos

THE RUDOLPH APARTMENT

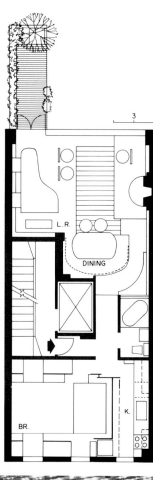

Overlooking the East River in New York City is a most remarkable apartment which owner Paul Rudolph uses as much as a design laboratory as a place of abode. Its measured spaces are confounded by mirrored surfaces in the bedroom that throw reflected images back and forth in an endless cadence and catch the images, real and reflected, of light screens that Rudolph uses to animate the space. Separated from the bedroom by a narrow entry hall lined in green plastic is the living area that opens through a glass window wall to the river. This space is lined on two walls by low, upholstered platforms adapted at intervals with backrests for seating. A grand piano, its legs let into the platform, occupies one wall. Across from it is a fireplace, only the upper portion of the opening visible over the platform. Curling overhead in a long, unifying arc are bookshelves that form a visual soffit.

The floor heights are modulated by gentle steps. At night the floors glow with bands of light and walls are washed by recessed fixtures. To those bred to a stark minimalism, the Rudolph apartment, with its obvious concern for form and texture, its abundance of richness and elaboration, may seem fussy and self-indulgent. Most readers, however, will see incipient design ideas—ideas about lighting, about storage about the manipulation of surface, some of which will find their way into larger building applications. Those that do not work will be replaced in this apartment by other experiments that are just as inventive.

RUDOLPH APARTMENT, New York City. Architect and owner: *Paul Rudolph.* Contractor: *Owner.*

THE SEAMAN/CROXTON APARTMENTS

Two apartments and the architects' own offices share a Beaux Arts townhouse, a consistent design language, and a contemporary elegance that fits their context well. Although the first two floors of the turn-of-the-century building had been completely remodeled by McKim, Mead and White in 1917, a subsequent conversion to apartments left only isolated details from grander times. Accordingly, the architects—much of whose work is concerned with preservation—were able to extensively revise floor plans and to plan around existing elements in a thoroughly new manner, with a clear conscience.

In the ground floor apartment designed for Mr. and Mrs. Thomas Seaman (isometric and photos on this page), only the living room with its ceiling moldings and fireplace survived intact. And this became the focus around which spaces were altered not only for functional reasons, but to bring the living room into a better formal relationship with the rest. Two small spaces at the entrance (bottom of isometric) were combined into one large kitchen, dining and entry area with a tile floor. A Renaissance relief that belonged to the owners was mounted on the low division wall between living and entry area, and serves as an eye-diverting focus before entering the living room itself. The living room has been painted a strong terra cotta color to emphasize its importance. Elsewhere in the apartment, partitions have been removed to provide a study adjacent to the living room and a large bath.

Architect Randolph Croxton's own apartment (photos and isometric on the opposite page) has a plan similar to the Seaman apartment, although the divisions between kitchen (bottom photo) and entry and between living room and study have been purposely accentuated instead of reduced. The wall between the living room and the study (sometimes used as a dining room, as in the photo) was thickened by the addition of bookcases. Ceiling moldings and the marble surfaces around the fireplace were the only original elements left in the living room when Croxton moved in. According to Croxton: "It was not easy to detail the fireplace and surrounding cabinetry to look like it had always been there." In the architectural offices (see following page), the small floor area has been utilized to the utmost to produce efficiency and a simultaneous feeling of spaciousness. Indeed, in all of the spaces, there is a tight arrangement of elements that capitalizes on the airiness of the larger rooms where they do exist.

THE SEAMAN AND CROXTON RESIDENCES AND THE CROXTON COLLABORATIVE OFFICES, New York, New York. Architects: *The Croxton Collaborative—project architect: Randolph R. Croxton; associate-in-charge: John T. Obelenus.* Lighting consultant: *Carroll Cline.*

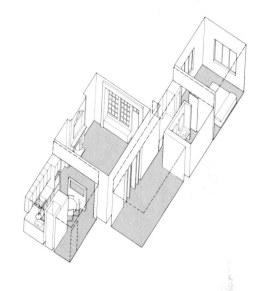

Otto Baitz photos

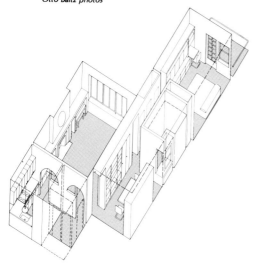

133

THE VIGNELLI APARTMENT

The apartment opens with a flourish. The front door, on the second floor of the duplex, leads onto a mezzanine overlooking the double-height living room with its high, arched, small-paned window. The Vignellis have played up the spectacular qualities of this echoing hall by cleansing the space, removing a partition on the lower floor and inserting a new staircase, tucked behind a cedilla-shaped wall. In this clear space, objects look brillant. The Vignelli-designed Saratoga couches (1964), the Quattro Cilindi marble coffee table (1979), or the aluminum steel cylinders originally designed as book-shelf supports, but here used purely as forms (1965), become sculpture.

New York designers Massimo and Lella Vignelli have made their apartment both showroom and home. They have transformed a large duplex in a 1909 Upper East Side apartment building into a series of classic Modern rooms, furnished throughout with the objects and furniture for which they are famous. The result — a strongly stated, purposely unresolved dialectic of extroversion and intimacy — provides a frame for both dramatic and daily action.

Norman McGrath photos

The dining room, which opens off the rear of the living room and, via a small passage, off the library, is a space whose austere bareness throws the objects it contains into sharper relief. Originally a plain box, with a small fireplace on one wall and the Vignelli's assemblable Quattro Cilindi table in the center, it has been transformed into an elegant dining hall by the insertion of two mirrors flanking the protruding fireplace. By elongating perceived space, the mirrors confer dignity on what is actually a relatively simple room, adding an element of sophisticated ambiguity and intrigue to the space (above, Massimo Vignelli in the dining room).

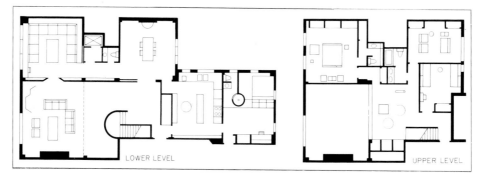

LOWER LEVEL   UPPER LEVEL

Just as one test of a design is "can you live with it?", so one test of a designer in his/her own home. Has he gutted the interior, uprooting walls to leave "spaces," or has he sheltered his privacy in conventional rooms? Does he furnish the place with those chairs he designed for Knoll, or does he go for the unimpeachable Barcelona? Does he drink from those cups with the ungrippable handles he designed for Heller, or does he serve those to his guests, himself sipping comfortably from a heavy, chipped china mug?

Many designers turn it all off so they can sleep at night, but Massimo and Lella Vignelli live with their designs round the clock. Their apartment illustrates their talent for composing carefully elaborated settings, frames for variegated action. Yet these interiors are flexible as well as fashionable; stylish, certainly, but not over-stylized.

Even at home, the Vignellis are always designers. They use the apartment for the various scales of entertainment crucial to their careers. Furnished with their designs, their apartment is showroom as well as home.

The design addresses this dual program by compartmentalizing functions. Clearly influenced by the Vignelli's experience in exhibition design, the design of their apartment treats each room as a separate installation, featuring an activity and their designs for it. The design is an analysis of a home, breaking down daily life into component episodes. It seeks to isolate, not integrate, these; to define the parts of this sequence, not to fuse them.

Public and private areas are carefully distinguished. Where the former are hard-edged spaces that preserve all their sharp right angles, the latter are softly outlined and the junction of vertical and horizontal in them is slightly blurred. Where the former clear space around focal objects (a table, a group of couches) the latter tend to push the objects to the edges, leaving the center to be filled by people. Where the public rooms are expanded by real or illusionary vistas opened into adjoining spaces, the private rooms are contracted, turned inward, their windows and doors all but eliminated.

This clear definition of individual *rooms*, each with its own particular character, recognizes the context in which the Vignelli's intervention takes place. In stressing the idea of self-contained volumes, defined by strong walls, the Vignellis have elicited the expressive potential of the massive masonry apartment building. Walls are shown to be thick, ceilings demonstrably heavy. Doors and windows force-

The jewel-like quality of the living room is sharply contrasted in the adjacent library (below). Entered through a narrowing slit of a door (above) that emphasizes the act of passage, the library is a warm, almost womb-like shelter. The Belgian linen which covers the couches, wall, windows and shelves envelops the tranquil, evenly lit room in a soft wrapping. Arranged in symmetrical pairs, standard light fixtures become geometric sculpture.

The guest room (above), a linen tent, was created out of a garret. In their son Luca's room (below) carpeted, stepped platforms forming sleeping and sitting areas are punctuated by a huge ''column'' anchoring the end of a partition. The cylinder, which marks the entrance to the bath, contains a shower.

fully violate these dense, solid cases in'
punching through them. The emphasized weight of the shell plays it up as a
"found object," an old carapace
invested with new activity.

This evocation and transformation
of the defining qualities of the existing
building describes, in a subtle layering
of contrasts and comparisons, both the
modernity of the Vignelli's design and
its simultaneous classicality. The light
beige walls, naked save for baseboard
and molding, the carpetless light wood
floors, throw into high relief the pure
geometry of the furniture (mostly the
Vignelli's earlier, more severe work). At
the same time, the sand finish of those
walls and the parquet fitting of the
floor, sanded so that every peg and
plank shows, heightens the presence,
the density of the structural divisions by
emphasizing their texture.

Furnishings and furniture delve into
the material of which they are made in
a similar fashion. The library, for example, mines possible meanings of natural-
colored Belgian linen in the seating,
wall, and window coverings. The Quattro Cilindi table at its center takes wood
as its subject; the door-sized plank lies
on log-shaped cylinders—or can be fitted into their ends so that they become
columns, the plank a roof. The object
changes form in response to its context; the low table is sunk into the
pillowy library, while the high version is
erected amid the perpendicular planes
of the dining room.

We, too, moving from room to
room, respond to this alternation of
hard and soft, open and closed, public
and private, void and solid, positive
and negative. The strictly maintained
duality establishes, as it were, two axes
in terms of which our motion is plotted
and invited.

One of the Vignelli's early posters
for the Museum of Modern Art, New
York, states in two dimensions what
their apartment states in four. In this
poster, heavy black horizontal lines car-
ry the information, while vertical separations group it into categories.
Through the center, in gravity-defying
stopped motion, leaps Fred Astaire,
clicking his heels at the top of his
hyperbolic trajectory. Human activity
sparks geometry. In the Vignelli's apartment, as in their work, it is we (or the
Vignellis) who activate the design by
moving within it, providing the curve
that gives the encompassing grid direction and meaning.

VIGNELLI APARTMENT, New York, New
York. Architects: *Massimo and Lella Vignelli.*
Lighting consultant: *Howard Brandston.*
Contractor: *John LaBarca.*

The intimacy of the library (above) is
intensified in the master bedroom
(below). Here Belgian linen pads even
the ceiling, cabinets, and window (as
a heavy drapery). A few crisp-edged
black, Vignelli-designed objects—the
Saratoga bed (1970), the Metaphora I
table (1979) maintain the horizontal
and vertical lines.

7

Houses designed to take advantage of the sun: still experimental, but offering a new and important way of living

Energy conservation is, of course, a subject of immense importance these days—as fuel costs become higher, it seems, with almost every passing month. And these higher and higher fuel costs constantly change the arithmetic of using solar energy to heat a house: the more conventional fuels cost, the more money that can be justified in first costs to build a house that uses less fuel because it makes effective use of all that free energy that pours in from the sun.

And higher first costs there are, make no mistake. For while energy from the sun is free, it is of course not available all of the time, and even a house designed with the most "active technology"—extensive solar collectors, for example—must also have a conventional heating system for the inevitable stretches of sunless weather. And it is still difficult—despite concentrated research by university research teams, the Department of Housing and Urban Development, the American Institute of Architects' Research Corporation, and individual architects and engineers—to predict in advance just how effective a solar heating system will be—what percentage of the needed heat input to a house will be provided by the solar technology.

And because of the "still-in-experiment" nature of solar design, it seems particularly appropriate for architects who are fascinated by the implications and opportunities of solar energy to try their ideas in the laboratory of their own houses—and that is just what the architects of the three houses in this chapter have done.

Only one of the houses—architect Larry Yaw's house in Colorado— is in a location especially favored for use of solar energy; there is a very high percentage of sunny winter days in that beautiful state, and a very high percentage of Coloradans (perhaps because of the beauty of their state) seem to have a very strong interest in the technology of conserving energy. (In Colorado, many schools and other large buildings have been designed around solar-energy technology.) The other two houses are in the Northeast —one in Princeton, New Jersey and the other in Greenwich, Connecticut— where it is harder to make the higher-first-cost/lower-fuel-cost arithmetic work out. But it can work out:

The Yaw house in Aspen—of course a major ski resort—reportedly obtains "75 percent of annual space heating requirements, 100 percent of domestic hot water requirements, as well as most of the energy needed for the outdoor hot tub" from its extensive array of solar collectors. These collectors are integrated into the design very effectively in the Yaw house (and managing that requires, make no mistake, very careful design). Further, the house is designed to be almost closed to the north—indeed a massive stone wall on the north is not just protection from weather, but serves as a heat-storage "mass." On the south, the sun is invited in all winter by large glass areas. With its extensive systems, this house uses what is called "active solar technology."

An example of a "passive" solar system is architect Renato Severino's house in Connecticut. It has very little solar "hardware"—but the way the house is shaped and the way its windows are set in, solar energy is expected to account for 30 percent of heating needs. In this exceedingly contemporary design, the huge sloping roof faces south, and the sun is invited in through an array of windows, some set with mirrors that bounce winter sunlight deep into the spaces but can be closed against summer heat. The triangular shape of the house also permits a very efficient "heat re-use" system—natural convection concentrates warm air at the point of the roof from where, any time the temperature there reaches 70 degrees, a fan pushes it through ducts back to the lower floors. (In summer, the hot air is simply exhausted to the outside.) Again, to minimize heat loss, the north wall is closed, and the two end walls are nearly closed. And so, again, this is a "passive solar house"—taking advantage of simple natural principles in the cause of energy conservation.

Perhaps the most "technological" of the three is the Kelbaugh house in Princeton, New Jersey. In this house, the primary "solar hardware" is a massive concrete wall—called a Trombe wall—set six inches behind a south-facing glass curtain wall. As air travels by convection in the narrow air space, it is heated and re-enters the room through openings for "windows" and a narrow space at the top. This system—in its first (and admittedly mild) winter accounted for 75 percent of heating for the house—the gas furnace and back-up infra-red heaters were little used. There are a number of things about this house that architect Kelbaugh says he would do differently—but again it is to the credit of architects who make this kind of commitment that they are learning with their own houses. Which is one of the things good architects do....

THE YAW HOUSE

Set into a south-facing bluff over the Roaring Fork River, where it commands a postcard-perfect view of Aspen slopes and the high Rockies above, architect Larry Yaw's house for his family of six exploits its surroundings with pragmatism and imagination.

"The design," Yaw says, "responds to three major goals: optimize solar orientation and exposure to accommodate maximum active and passive solar heating systems; integrate regional forms and materials with the high tech expression of solar hardware; and create, from the steeply sloping site, usable exterior spaces for outdoor activity."

The organization of the house around two long parallel forms, connected at the upper level by a "bridge" element, provides long south-facing surfaces for solar purposes. The residual space between, used as entry and play area, reasserts the nature in which the built forms are placed.

Inside, the traditional functional organization—social and family areas on the lower level, sleeping and private areas above—is enlivened by emphasized connections to outdoor areas and interior openings that enlarge the space.

By extending the solar collectors on their triangular support forms beyond the enclosed volumes, the design not only increases collector area but also protects the exterior decks on both ends of each long element. The solar profile of the south facade, accented by bright red terminations of the collector banks, acts in counterpoint to the gently sloped, cottage-like shingle roofs of the north facade, which tie the building into the wooded uphill slope.

Glazed openings are concentrated on the south; only three small "diamond" windows, sheltered by gables, peer out of the north side. In contrast to the other exterior walls, of gray-stained lapped cedar siding, the north walls are made of

concrete "rubble" using stone found near the site. The stone wall creates thermal mass and protects the house from heavy winter snows. Thoroughly integrated into the design's esthetic, the active and passive solar systems are relatively simple; their major components are, respectively, down-drain water collectors and south-facing glazed openings. But together they account for 75 per cent of the annual space heating requirements and 100 per cent of the heated domestic water, as well as most of the energy needed for the outdoor hot tub.

Yaw's is a house in the best American tradition: common-sensical yet ingenious in function, "self-made" yet sophisticated in form.

Architects: Copland, Hagman, Yaw Ltd.
    210 South Galena Street
    Aspen, Colorado
Owners: Mr. and Mrs. Larry Yaw
Engineers: Anderson and Hastings (structural)
    Lincoln-Devore (foundation)
    McFall, Konkel and Kimball (mechanical).
Contractor: Sutherland Construction Co.

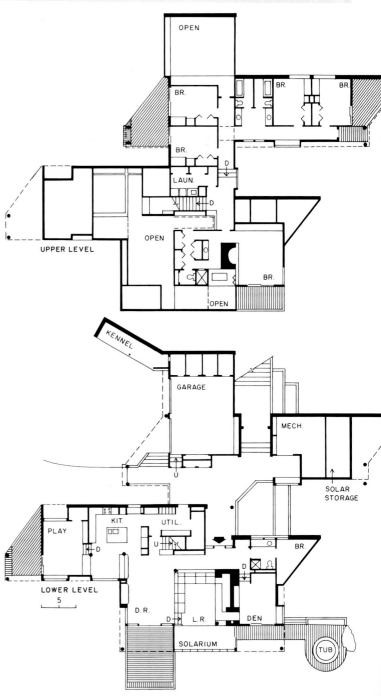

UPPER LEVEL

OPEN

BR.

BR.

BR.

BR.

LAUN.

D

D

OPEN

BR.

OPEN

KENNEL

GARAGE

MECH.

SOLAR
STORAGE

LOWER LEVEL
5

PLAY

KIT.

UTIL.

U

BR.

D

D.R.

L.R.

DEN

D

SOLARIUM

TUB

The natural setting is allowed to permeate the house; the living-dining area, play room, den and four of the five bedrooms open directly onto a deck. Family areas are articulated with permeable divisions—columns, a change in floor height, built-in cabinets—so as to demarcate, not partition, the space, and allow it to be shared visually as it is in terms of activity. Architectural artifacts, such as a cast-iron Corinthian column, flavor the interior with eccentric wit.

THE SEVERINO HOUSE

A white stucco right triangle is not an obvious choice for a house on a hilltop in stately Greenwich with views of Long Island Sound. It is a choice that bears some examination.

The triangular shape developed from passive solar energy considerations being given pre-eminence in the design process: the heavily-glazed main roof facade—the hypotenuse of the triangle—faces south at a 45 degree angle for optimum sun infiltration; the north elevation is sheer, perpendicular, with only narrow strips of windows. It is an especially straightforward, logical parti, inviting comparison to a traditional New England saltbox.

The more curious question is why the execution of the triangular form—especially the east and west elevations—has been honed to the point of austerity. This raises the topical issues of esthetic preference and of a building's appropriateness to its context. Architect Renato Severino wanted the house to have a geometric precision that would give it "intensity." And for Severino, intensity translates into a strict articulation of form, best left unmitigated by softened edges. The choice of white stucco accentuates and purifies the geometry of the form.

This house raises two questions: whether the accommodation of solar energy is a sufficient premise on which to base a design, and whether an architecture of intensity is appropriate in the context of a traditional neighborhood. Both questions seem especially well-timed, and it is a measure of Renato Severino's conviction that he chose his own house as a forum for his investigations.

SEVERINO RESIDENCE, Greenwich, Connecticut. Architect: *Renato Severino, Architects & Planners*—principal-in-charge: *Renato Severino; assistant: Michael Kreindler.*

Norman McGrath photos

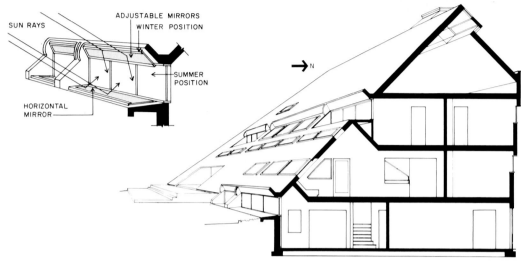

SUN RAYS

ADJUSTABLE MIRRORS
WINTER POSITION

SUMMER POSITION

HORIZONTAL MIRROR

N →

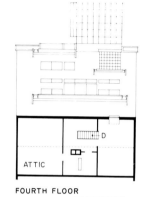

ATTIC

D

FOURTH FLOOR

BR

BR

U D

BR

THIRD FLOOR

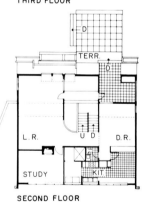

D

TERR.

D

L.R.

U D

D.R.

STUDY

KIT.

SECOND FLOOR

FAMILY

HOBBY

U

BR

GAR.

GAR.

FIRST FLOOR

5

The interior of the house presents a duality between the openness of the public spaces—with much emphasis on the play of light and the framing of unconventional views—and the simple, almost common rooms on the north side of the house. Architect Severino considers the triangular form of the house especially logical because it invites natural convection, drawing heat up to the attic where in the winter thermostatically-controlled fans recirculate warm air back through the house once it reaches 70 degrees, and where in the summer heat is discharged through vents in the roof. The intention was to design a house that would allow for 30 per cent of the total energy requirements to be met by a combination of solar collectors and a natural passive system that uses operable "roof windows" with adjustable mirrors to control heat reception year round.

THE KELBAUGH HOUSE

The Kelbaugh house is a 2100-square-foot, year-round residence in suburban Princeton, a community with a 40 degree north latitude, a climate that typically includes 5100 heating degree days, and a 50-55 per cent sunshine factor during the winter.

By obtaining a zoning variance, the Kelbaughs were able to push the house to the northern boundary of their 60- by 100-foot lot, thus clearing the pattern of shadows cast by neighboring houses and at the same time, giving the lot an ample outdoor space instead of the usual mishmash of shallow yards.

The key to the solar capabilities of the design is the massive concrete wall, an adaptation of the "Trombe wall" (see section drawing) set back six inches from the glass curtain wall that faces south. The 600-square-foot concrete surface absorbs and stores heat from the sun and radiates it continually into living spaces that are nearly uninterrupted spatially both upstairs and down. Back-up space heating has been provided by a gas-fired, hot air system, independent of the house's solar capabilities, but with ductwork cast into the concrete wall.

During its first winter (a mild one with about 4500 degree days), the Kelbaugh house performed well. With the thermostat for the back up system set in the 60-64 F range (58 F at night), only 338 cubic feet of natural gas was consumed. This represented a saving of nearly 75 per cent when compared with the estimated 1220 cubic feet of gas that would have been required to maintain a 65 F daytime temperature by conventional heating. And these savings came at little sacrifice to comfort. The temperatures inside were allowed to swing 3-6 degrees during the 24-hour cycle to allow the concrete wall to collect and discharge its heat. Auxiliary 250-watt infrared heaters were installed in the bathroom but seldom needed and the fireplace was used several times a week for localized comfort.

Insulation, of course, is critical. Kelbaugh provided an average 4-inch wall insulation of cellulosic fiber (recycled newspaper) and a 9½-inch roof insulation that achieved an R factor of 40. In addition, he used a one-inch thickness of polystyrene (two inches would have been better, he reports) on the perimeter foundation wall to a depth of two feet. The re-

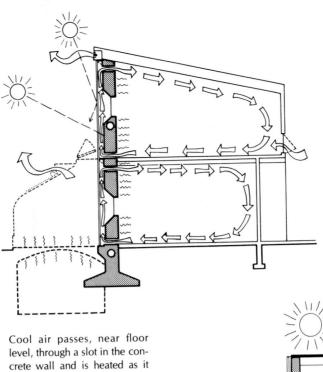

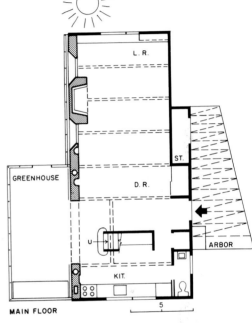

Cool air passes, near floor level, through a slot in the concrete wall and is heated as it rises through the narrow space between the glazing and the wall. It re-enters the space through slots at ceiling height. Circulation through the room is by gravity convection. In summer, the narrow space is vented at the eave. When gravity convection does not suffice, four small fans are employed.

MAIN FLOOR

sultant heat loss, by conventional analysis is about 75,000 Btu per hour—32,000 of which is lost to the small greenhouse on the south face of the building. After double glazing this greenhouse, and fitting it with rolling shades, the loss should be considerably less next winter. Other adjustments and fine tuning will follow to balance temperature differentials between upstairs and down. With refreshing candor, Kelbaugh says that if he was beginning again, he would enlarge the eave vents and/or install operable windows in the south wall to increase cross ventilation.

As the photos amply indicate, the Kelbaugh house is much more than just a struggle for energy efficiency. Though it is frankly experimental, it is nonetheless a tightly disciplined piece of design with the kind of apparent simplicity that only comes with close study and careful refinement. Questions raised by its presence among the more indulgent residential forms of the past must be measured against the lessons it can yield to those interested in a less energy-extravagant future.

KELBAUGH HOUSE, Princeton, New Jersey. Architect: *Douglas Kelbaugh*. Contractor: *Nathan Bard*.

Robert Perron photos

The greenhouse, through which about half the heat loss of the house occurs, experiences a wide fluctuation in diurnal temperatures. Kelbaugh has taken steps to stabilize this condition by double glazing the wall and will add drums filled with water to retain further heat. The drums will double as plant stands.

A final word on "solar houses..."

They are, as the houses in this chapter have shown, still experimental. These are three of the handsomest solar houses yet designed—in many, the hardware of solar collection is not nearly as well integrated into the house design as in these three. Before embarking on a house of solar design—if your convictions lead you in that direction and your part of the country has a suitable amount of sunshine year-round—study the literature of solar houses carefully. Be realistic in your expectations. And retain an architect who has worked with solar design...or at least studied it carefully.

The design techniques and systems must still be considered experimental—though the experience bank grows with each new project, with every year. And perhaps someday soon a great many of us can enjoy the benefits of good solar design—reveling not just in the lower costs of operating our houses, but in the conviction that we are contributing to a whole new less-energy-extravagant way of living. Which is one of the things all of us should be doing....

Where to find the architects whose houses are featured in this book

CHAPTER THREE

"Larger houses for larger sites: some shaped by their sites, some giving shape to the ubiquitous flat site..."

CHAPTER FOUR

"Vacation houses: houses designed for a relaxed kind of living often generate a very special kind of design excitement..."

CHAPTER FIVE

"Houses for hot climates: two desert houses and a sub-tropical island house which explore ways to live comfortably when it is very hot ... which of course can occur almost anywhere ..."

p. 111
Fred Linn Osmon
P.O. Box 1454
Carefree, Arizona 85377

p. 114
William P. Bruder
Box 4575
New River Stage
New River, Arizona 85029

p. 117
Harry Bates
36 N. Hollow Drive
East Hampton, Long Island, New York 11937

CHAPTER SIX

"Apartments designed by architects for their own use offer some special lessons in the use of space ..."

p. 121
Ulrich Franzen
555 Madison Avenue
New York, New York 10022

p. 124
Alan Buchsbaum
Design Coalition
12 Greene Street
New York, New York 10013

p. 128
Michael Rubin
Rubin/Smith-Miller
305 Canal Street
New York, New York 10013

p. 130
Paul Rudolph
54 West 57th Street
New York, New York 10019

p. 132
Randolph R. Croxton
Croxton Collaborative
16 East 84th Street
New York, New York 10028

p. 134
Vignelli Associates
410 East 62nd Street
New York, New York 10021

CHAPTER SEVEN
"Houses designed to take advantage of solar energy: still experimental, still handsome is as handsome does. But fascinating..."

p. 142

Copland, Hagman, Yaw Ltd.
210 South Galena Street
Suite 24
Aspen, Colorado 81611

p. 146

Renato Severino
8 Greenwich Avenue
Greenwich, Connecticut 06830

p. 150

Douglas Kelbaugh
Kelbaugh & Lee Architects
240 Nassau Street
Princeton, New Jersey 08540

Index